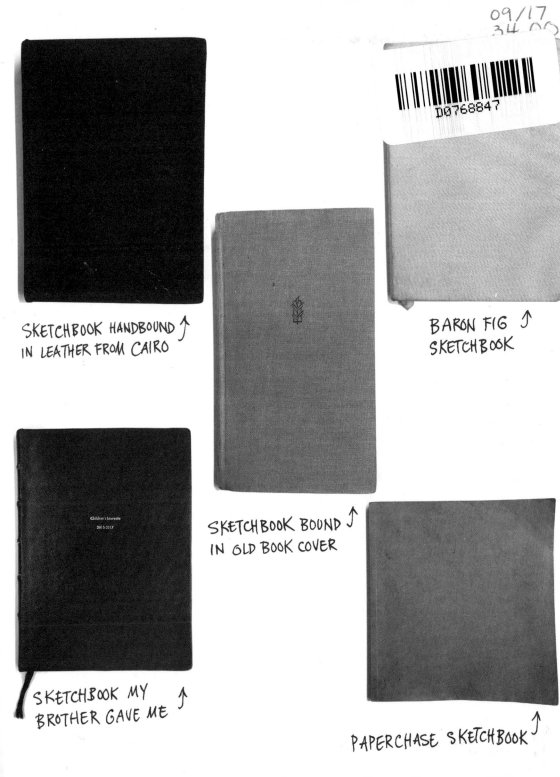

09/17
34.00

D0768847

SKETCHBOOK HANDBOUND ↑
IN LEATHER FROM CAIRO

BARON FIG ↑
SKETCHBOOK

SKETCHBOOK BOUND ↑
IN OLD BOOK COVER

SKETCHBOOK MY ↑
BROTHER GAVE ME

PAPERCHASE SKETCHBOOK ↑

Travels with My Sketchbook

Chris Riddell, Children's Laureate 2015–2017, is an accomplished artist and political cartoonist for the *Observer*. His books have won many awards, including the 2001, 2004 and 2016 CILIP Kate Greenaway Medals, the Nestlé Children's Book Prize and the Red House Children's Book Award. *Goth Girl and the Ghost of a Mouse* won the Costa Children's Book Award in 2013.

Travels with My Sketchbook

Chris Riddell

Children's Laureate 2015–2017

MACMILLAN

First published 2017 by Macmillan Children's Books
an imprint of Pan Macmillan
20 New Wharf Road, London N1 9RR
Associated companies throughout the world
www.panmacmillan.com

ISBN 978-1-5098-5656-5

Chris Riddell will donate all royalties from this book to BookTrust.

To find out more about BookTrust you can visit
www.booktrust.org.uk

Introduction

The Children's Laureate is a position awarded once every two years to a writer or illustrator to promote and encourage children's interest in literature and reading, and stemmed from a conversation between the Poet Laureate Ted Hughes and children's writer Michael Morpurgo almost twenty years ago.

As the ninth Children's Laureate I have travelled far and wide, and wherever I have gone I have taken a sketchbook and drawn sketches of what I have been up to. Compiling these drawings into this book has been a great pleasure and has reminded me not only of the thousands of people I have met and the huge range of very varied events I have attended, but also of the seismic world events of the past two years. I have included illustrations, political cartoons, card games and poems, all of which I have drawn over the hectic two years of my laureateship. I feel profoundly changed by my time as Laureate and it has been a great joy and honour to campaign on behalf of young readers. I will continue to fight for libraries and champion illustrators once I have passed on the baton in June.

I want to thank everyone who has supported me in my travels – BookTrust, Waterstones, Macmillan Children's Books, the *Observer* newspaper, librarians everywhere and my long-suffering and ever loyal wife, Princess Joanna of Norfolk.

CHRIS RIDDELL

CHRIS RIDDELL

IT BEGINS...

THE SKETCHBOOK MY MOTHER GAVE ME

JUNE 2015

LOADING MY LAUREATE LUGGAGE ON MY METAPHORICAL MULE READY FOR A LONG JOURNEY...

THIS AFTERNOON BUMPED INTO MY FAVOURITE BRIGHTON BAND THE LEISURE SOCIETY JUST AFTER POSTING A DRAWING ILLUSTRATING ONE OF THEIR SONGS...

HAVING A LOVELY INTERVIEW WITH MICHELLE FROM THE GUARDIAN AND HER BABY DAUGHTER FINISTÈRE...

MAJOR GENERAL MORPEACEFUL

THE BIG FRIENDLY GENIUS

HERE I AM TAKING OVER FROM MALORIE BLACKMAN AND BECOMING THE NINTH UK CHILDREN'S LAUREATE

GRIZZLYMIKE THE BEAR HUNTER

THE SILVER SIGNER

EXTREMELY FINE ANNE

ANTHONY LORD OF THE APES

JULIA THE GRUFFALO TAMER

THE INCREDIBLE NOUGHT & CROSSER

THE DOODLER

I WORE THIS MASK FOR A NUMBER OF VISITS TO WATERSTONES BOOK SHOPS TO DRAW ON THEIR WALLS BUT I KEPT BEING RECOGNISED...

3

9TH JUNE 2015

MEDIA MEANDERINGS

GETTING MATT TO DOODLE ON CHANNEL FIVE

BAFTA CHILDREN'S LAUREATE RECEPTION...

BIG HUGS

FEELING THE LOVE.

TWIRLING WITH LOVELY NEWSROUND

INTERROGATED BY YOUNG GUARDIAN REVIEWERS

IN A RADIO CAR TALKING TO BBC RADIO 4 WORLD AT ONE AND 5 LIVE

TOASTING THIS EXTRAORDINARY DAY

CHEERS!

CHEERS!

ON THE FRONT ROW WITH JOHN WILSON

WITH MY GOOD FRIEND, MR. PAN MACMILLAN

5

WEARING MY
POLITICAL CARTOONIST
HAT TODAY, WORKING
ON SUNDAY'S
OBSERVER
CARTOON

12TH JUNE 2015

13TH JUNE 2015

KURETAKE 'MILLION YEAR' WRITING BRUSH

THE MYSTERIOUS MASKED MAN 'THE DOODLER' MAKES HIS DEBUT AT BRIGHTON WATERSTONES

LEGAL DOCUMENT SIGNED BY 'A. JAMES DAUNT' GIVING DOODLE PERMISSION!

WATERSTONES WALL

WATERSTONES WINDOW

WATERSTONES SEAT

INNOCENT BYSTANDERS

MICHELE FROM DAVE'S COMICS

NICKY SINGER THE WRITER

RICH FROM WATERSTONES

EXCELLENT COFFEE

THIS IS WHERE I MET THE WRITER NICKY SINGER AND WE DECIDED TO WORK TOGETHER ON 'ISLAND' SEE PAGE 21

16TH JUNE -2015-

LIFE CAST I BOUGHT FROM THE MUSEUM SHOP AT THE TATE IN 1985.

SPENDING TIME IN THE STUDIO WATCHED OVER BY THE KINDLY SPIRIT OF WILLIAM BLAKE

17TH JUNE -2015-

SADDLING UP MY METAPHORICAL MULE AND TROTTING TO MEET WITH MY VERY GOOD FRIEND, THE WISE WIZARD GAIMAN TO FILM IN THE MYTHICAL KINGDOM OF BATTERSEA

HUBRIS

EURO NIGHTMARES

DRAWING
MYTHOLOGICAL
NIGHTMARES
FOR SUNDAY'S
OBSERVER

19TH
JUNE
2015

GREXIT

Illustrating the cover of
The Literary
Review
ON
DUELLING

20TH
JUNE
—2015—

Literary Review

JULY 2015 Issue 433 £3.95

www.literaryreview.co.uk

Duel Identities
Jonathan Keates

STALIN'S REBEL DAUGHTER
Donald Rayfield

INDIA AGAINST THE AXIS
John Keay

SOVIET BLOCKS
Jonathan Meades

BEING MRS CHURCHILL
Jane Ridley

RAID ON ENTEBBE • YOGA COMES TO HOLLYWOOD • GAME OF DRONES
A GAUCHO IN LONDON • BUCKLEY VS MAILER • TOO MUCH TECHINT?

9 770144 436072

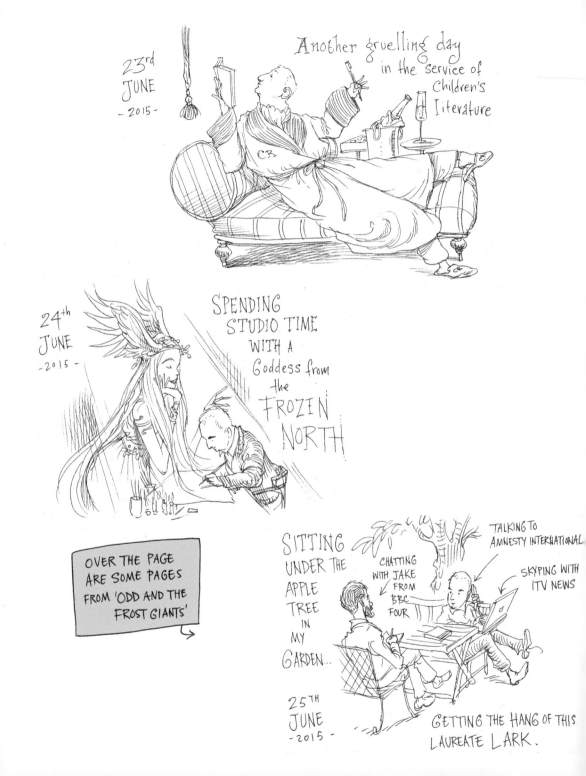

CHAPTER ONE
Odd

CHAPTER ONE
Odd

There was a boy called Odd, and there was nothing strange or unusual about that, not in that time or place. Odd meant *the tip of a blade*, and it was a lucky name.

He *was* odd though. At least, the other villagers thought so. But if there was one thing that he wasn't, it was lucky.

His father had been killed during a sea-raid, two years before, when Odd was ten. It was not unknown for people to get killed in sea-raids, but his father wasn't killed by a Scotsman, dying in glory in the heat of battle as a Viking should. He had jumped overboard to rescue one of the stocky little ponies that they took with them on their raids as pack animals.

They would load the ponies up with all the gold and valuables and food and weapons that they could find, and the ponies would trudge back to the longship. The ponies were the most valuable and hard-working things on the ship. After Olaf the Tall was killed by a Scotsman, Odd's father had to look after the ponies. Odd's father wasn't very experienced with ponies, being a woodcutter and woodcarver by trade, but he did his best. On the return journey, one of the ponies got loose, during a squall off Orkney, and fell overboard. Odd's father jumped into the grey sea with a rope, pulled the pony back to the ship and, with the other Vikings, hauled it back up on deck.

11

'The Giant wanted Freya, most lovely of the Goddesses.'

'Aye. Gods,' said the bear. 'I was just getting to that. I am great Thor, Lord of the Thunders. The eagle is Lord Odin, All-Father, Greatest of the Gods. And this runt-eared meddling fox is –'

'Loki,' said the fox smoothly. 'Blood brother to the Gods. Smartest, sharpest, most brilliant of all the inhabitants of Asgard, or so they say –'

'Brilliant?' snorted the bear.

'You would have fallen for it. Anyone would,' said the fox.

'Fallen for *what?*' said Odd.

A flash of green eyes, a sigh, and the fox began. 'I'll tell you. And you'll see. It could have happened to anyone. So, Asgard. Home of the mighty. In the middle of a plain, surrounded by an impregnable wall, built for us by a Frost Giant. And it was due to me, I should add, that that wall did not cost us the Giant's fee, which was unreasonably high.'

'Freya,' said the bear. 'The Giant wanted Freya. Most lovely of the Goddesses – with, obviously, the exception of Sif, my own little love. And it wanted the sun and the moon.'

'If you interrupt me one more time,' said the fox, '*one more time,* I will not only stop talking, but I shall go off on my own and leave the two of you to fend for yourselves.'

The bear said, 'Yes, but –'

'*Not one word.*'

The bear was silent.

The fox said, 'In the great hall of Odin sat all the Gods, drinking mead, eating and telling stories. They drank and bragged and fought and boasted and drank, all through the night and well into the small hours. The women had gone to bed hours since, and now the fires in the hall burned low and most of the Gods slept where they sat, heads resting on the wooden tables.

'I look like this anyway,' said Odd.

'I know,' said Freya She knelt down beside him, reached out a hand towards his injured leg. 'May I?'

'Um. If you want to.'

She picked him up as if he was light as a leaf, and put him down on the great feasting table of the Gods. She reached down to his right foot and deftly unhooked it at the knee. She ran a nail across the shin and the flesh parted. Freya looked at the bone, and her face fell. 'It was crushed,' she said. 'So much that not even I can repair it.' And then she said, 'But I can help.'

She pushed her hand into the inside of Odd's leg, kneading the smashed bones, pulling together the fragments from inside the leg, smoothing them together. Then she opened the flesh of the foot and repeated the same operation, putting the pieces of foot-bone and toe-bone back where they were meant to be. And then she encased the skeletal leg and foot in flesh once more, scaled it up, and the Goddess Freya reattached Odd's leg to Odd, and it was as if it had always been there.

'Sorry,' she said. 'I did the best I could do. It's better, but it's not right, yet.' She seemed lost in thought, then she said brightly, 'Why don't I replace it entirely? What about a cat's rear leg? Or a chicken's?'

Odd smiled, and shook his head. 'No thank you. This is good,' he said.

Odd stood up cautiously, put his weight on his right leg, trying to pretend he had not just seen his leg unhooked at the knee. He leaned on it. It did not hurt. Not really. Not like it used to.

'Give it time,' said Freya.

A huge hand came down and clapped Odd on the shoulder, sending him flying.

'Now, laddie,' boomed Thor. 'Tell us just how you defeated the might of the Frost Giants.' He seemed much more cheerful than when he had been a bear.

'There was only one of them,' said Odd.

'When *I* tell the story,' said Thor, 'there will be at least a dozen.'

'I want my shoes back,' said Loki.

27TH JUNE -2015-

I LEFT HANDED DEXTERITY

BOOK BUYER'S INSCRUTABLE STARE →

SIGNING BOOKS WITH MY GOOD FRIEND DANIEL WHELAN AT THE WONDERFUL CHILDREN'S BOOK SHOP IN MUSWELL HILL

THIS IS GRENDEL'S MOTHER IN HER LAIR, FROM BRIAN PATTEN'S RETELLING OF BEOWULF - "MONSTER SLAYER" →

28TH JUNE -2015-

REMEMBERING THE FIRST BOOK I WROTE AT THE BRILLIANT BEFORE BOOKFEST

MR. UNDERBED

BOOKES KATY

BOOKES RACHAEL

LOOKED AFTER WITH CHARM AND LAUGHTER BY KATY AND RACHAEL & EMMA from WATERSTONES

29TH JUNE 2015

Mrs. Grendel senior is paying me a visit in my studio today - I'll do my best to flatter her.

1ST JULY -2015-

Hottest day of the year so far...
Doing some laureate lolling about.

He hasn't moved for hours...

2nd JULY -2015-

SPENDING THE DAY WITH OLD FRIENDS

from The Edge Chronicles

THE BANDERBEAR IS ONE OF MY FAVOURITE CHARACTERS FROM THE EDGE CHRONICLES, A SERIES OF FANTASY NOVELS I CO-WROTE WITH THE WRITER PAUL STEWART

4TH JULY -2015-

A DAY OF EDGE CELEBRATIONS AT THE BOOK NOOK DAVE'S COMICS AND MY GARDEN

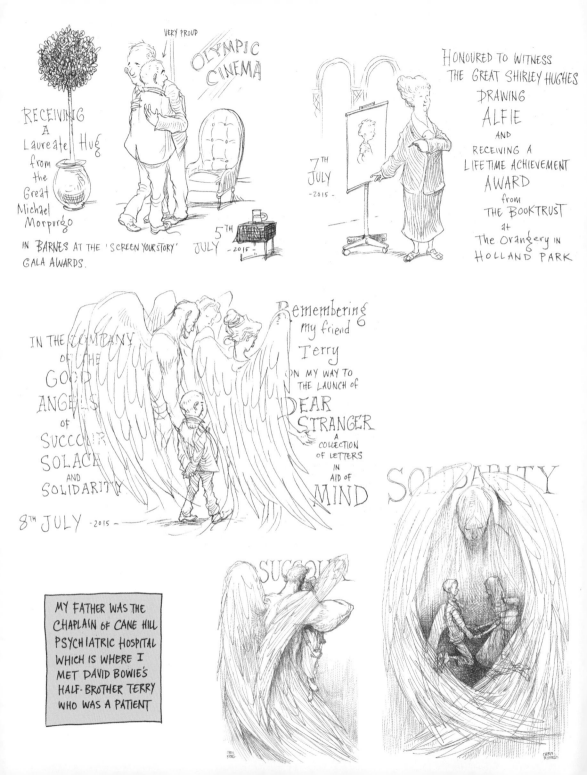

VERY PROUD

OLYMPIC CINEMA

RECEIVING A Laureate Hug from the Great Michael Morpurgo

IN BARNES AT THE 'SCREEN YOUR STORY' GALA AWARDS.

5TH JULY -2015-

HONOURED TO WITNESS THE GREAT SHIRLEY HUGHES DRAWING ALFIE AND RECEIVING A LIFETIME ACHIEVEMENT AWARD from THE BOOKTRUST at The Orangery IN HOLLAND PARK

7TH JULY -2015-

IN THE COMPANY OF THE GOOD ANGELS OF SUCCOUR SOLACE AND SOLIDARITY

8TH JULY -2015-

Remembering my friend Terry ON MY WAY TO THE LAUNCH OF DEAR STRANGER A COLLECTION OF LETTERS IN AID OF MIND

SOLIDARITY

SUCCOUR

MY FATHER WAS THE CHAPLAIN OF CANE HILL PSYCHIATRIC HOSPITAL WHICH IS WHERE I MET DAVID BOWIE'S HALF-BROTHER TERRY WHO WAS A PATIENT

9TH JULY -2015-

VISITING HERNE JUNIOR SCHOOL TO SEE THEIR 'CHRIS RIDDELL' PROJECT

THE LONG ARMS OF THE LAUREATE.

WHAT A FASCINATING SUBJECT...

← BE-MEDALLED

CHRIS RIDDELL

AN AMAZING WEEK... LOOKING FORWARD TO DOING IT ALL AGAIN NEXT WEEK...

10TH JULY -2015-

OFF TO THE Amazing Book Awards Tonight at the Shoreham Academy

11TH JULY -2015-

IN NEED OF A HAIRCUT AND A SHAVE.

LOTS OF PICTURES

VERY SHARP PENCIL

DRAWING WHAT I BELIEVE IS THE SECRET TO A GOOD CHILDREN'S BOOK AT THE BRIGHTON LAUNCH of *(verb not a Berkshire Town)* The Summer Reading Challenge at The JUBILEE LIBRARY

Being Guided by the Spirit of the Great Ice Bear

12TH JULY -2015-

A Flurry of illustrations

THIS IS THE COVER OF 'ISLAND' - A BEAUTIFUL ECO-FABLE

20

ISLAND

NICKY SINGER

CHATTING WITH A RANDOM PENGUIN AT THE SERPENTINE GALLERY THIS EVENING

13TH JULY
-2015-

Drawing Loki the crafty Fox today

15TH JULY

I LOVED ILLUSTRATING 'ODD AND THE FROST GIANTS' BY NEIL, AND LOKI WAS MY FAVOURITE NORSE GOD

GOING FULL TILT

JULY
16TH
-2015-

IN THE STUDIO TODAY

#LOVE DRAWING

23

21ST JULY
-2015-

DEADLINE TENTACLE

EXPLORING THE FAR FUTURE WITH MY FELLOW SCAVENGER AND VERY GOOD FRIEND PAUL STEWART

WHERE ON EARTH ARE WE

DON'T ASK ME...

Dancing a Jig of Delight

22nd JULY
-2015-

WITH Publisher of the Year Pan Macmillan

Working Immensely Hard

23rd JULY
-2015-

DEFINITELY NOT PUTTING MY FEET UP...

ON LAUREATE DUTIES

BILLOWS OF GOODWILL

24

Feeling gloomy about the Labour Party...

24TH JULY
-2015-

DRAWING MY CARTOON FOR
THE OBSERVER

MY THOUGHTS
ON THE LABOUR
PARTY HAVEN'T
CHANGED MUCH
SINCE I DREW
THIS!

25TH JULY - 2015 -

THINKING OF BOOK FILLED SHELVES AND THE WONDERFUL BUILDINGS THAT CONTAIN THEM...

CELEBRATE LIBRARIES

THIS IS A QUOTE FROM A SPEECH NEIL GAVE AT THE BRITISH LIBRARY

THEY WERE GOOD LIBRARIANS. THEY LIKED BOOKS AND THEY LIKED BOOKS BEING READ. THEY JUST SEEMED TO LIKE THAT THERE WAS THIS WIDE-EYED LITTLE BOY WHO LOVED TO READ, AND WOULD TALK TO ME ABOUT THE BOOKS I WAS READING, THEY WOULD FIND ME OTHER BOOKS... THEY WOULD HELP.

NEIL GAIMAN.

SUNDAY IN CYBERSPACE

26TH JULY - 2015 -

POST-IT NOTES ON THE WALL OF SMALL AIRLESS STUDY →

THE INFINITY OF SPACE

WRITING WITH MY GOOD FRIEND PAUL STEWART

TAP TAP TAP TAP TAP

Lunching with a Comic Phoenix

27TH JULY - 2015 -

'THE PHOENIX' IS A WONDERFUL CHILDREN'S COMIC PUBLISHED BY DAVID FICKLING BOOKS →

PLANNING SOME POETRY ADVENTURES...

IN MY NORFOLK STUDIO

30TH JULY - 2015 -

LETTING MY MIND WANDER

THE WAY THINGS ARE

No, THE CANDLE IS NOT CRYING, IT
CANNOT FEEL PAIN.

EVEN TELESCOPES, LIKE THE REST OF US,
GROW BORED.

BUBBLEGUM WILL NOT MAKE THE HAIR
SOFT AND SHINY.

THE DULLER THE IMAGINATION,
THE FASTER THE CAR,

I AM YOUR FATHER

AND THIS IS THE WAY THINGS
ARE.

WHEN THE SKY IS LOOKING THE
OTHER WAY,

DO NOT ENTER THE FOREST. NO, THE WIND

IS NOT CAUSED BY THE RUSHING
OF CLOUDS.

AN EXCUSE IS AS GOOD A REASON
AS ANY.

A LIGHTHOUSE, LAUNCHED, WILL NOT
GO FAR.

I AM YOUR FATHER

AND THIS IS THE WAY THINGS
ARE.

No, OLD PEOPLE DO NOT WALK SLOWLY
BECAUSE THEY HAVE PLENTY OF
TIME.

GARDENING BOOKS WHEN BURIED
WILL NOT FLOWER.

THOUGH LIGHTLY WORN, A CROWN MAY
LEAVE A SCAR.

I AM YOUR FATHER

AND THIS IS THE WAY THINGS
ARE.

No, THE RED WOOLLY HAT HAS NOT BEEN
PUT ON THE RAILING TO KEEP IT WARM.

WHEN ONE GLOVE IS MISSING,
BOTH ARE LOST.

TODAY'S CRAFT FAIR IS TOMORROW'S
CAR BOOT SALE.

THE GUITARIST GENTLY WEEPS,
NOT THE GUITAR,

I AM YOUR FATHER

AND THIS IS THE WAY THINGS
ARE.

PEBBLES WORK BEST WITHOUT
BATTERIES,

THE DECKCHAIR WILL FAIL
AS A UNIT OF CURRENCY.

EVEN THOUGH YOUR SHADOW IS
SHORTENING

IT DOES NOT MEAN YOU ARE GROWING
SMALLER.

MOONBEAMS SADLY, WILL NOT
SURVIVE IN A JAR.

I AM YOUR FATHER

AND THIS IS THE WAY THINGS
ARE.

FOR CENTURIES THE BULLET REMAINED
QUIETLY CONFIDENT

THAT THE GUN WOULD BE INVENTED.

A DROWNING DADAIST WILL NOT
APPRECIATE

THE CONCRETE LIFEBELT.

NO GUARANTEE MY LAST GOODBYE
IS AU REVOIR...

I AM YOUR FATHER

AND THIS IS THE WAY THINGS
ARE.

DO NOT BECOME A PRISON-OFFICER
UNLESS YOU KNOW
WHAT YOU'RE LETTING SOMEONE ELSE
IN FOR.
THE THRILL OF BEING A
SHOWER CURTAIN WILL SOON
PALL.

NO TRUSTING HAND AWAITS
THE FALLING
STAR,

I AM YOUR FATHER, AND
I'M SORRY,
BUT THIS IS THE WAY
THINGS ARE.

ROGER
McGOUGH

A
TIDE
OF
HUMAN MISERY

A
SV
ECON

COLLECTIVE

ARM

IC MIGRANTS

A
MURMUR
OF
UNSAVOURY INVESTORS

NOUNS

31ST
JULY
-2015-

DRAWING MY
OBSERVER CARTOON
IN MY COMFORTABLE,
SAFE STUDIO IN
NORFOLK WHILE HUMAN
TIDES OF MISERY
CONTINUE TO SWELL...

THE SERIOUS SEASON

BIGOTRY

RBS

TAX PAYERS MONEY

GOP

FRATRICIDE

SET ASIDE

POMICIDE

FEELING AUSSIE
CRICKET'S PAIN IN MY
OBSERVER CARTOON

7TH
AUGUST
—2015—

ASHES.

10TH AUGUST -2015-

Beached

Without MY INTERNET CONNECTION...

NO MORE SURFING UNTIL IT'S FIXED.

SPEEDING TOWARDS THE FINISH OF MY LATEST PROJECT...

A FEW NEW PROJECTS WAITING IN THE WINGS.

11TH AUGUST -2015-

12TH AUGUST -2015-

MY ILLUSTRATION HERO

Talking about the incomparable E.H. Shepard at The House of Illustration Today... WE BOTH WORKED FOR PUNCH Magazine.

AUTUMN

13TH AUGUST -2015-

DISGUISE

CRUMPLED JACKET

STRATEGIC PLANNING BACK IN THE DOODLE CAVE...

IT IS GOING TO BE A BUSY AUTUMN

34

35

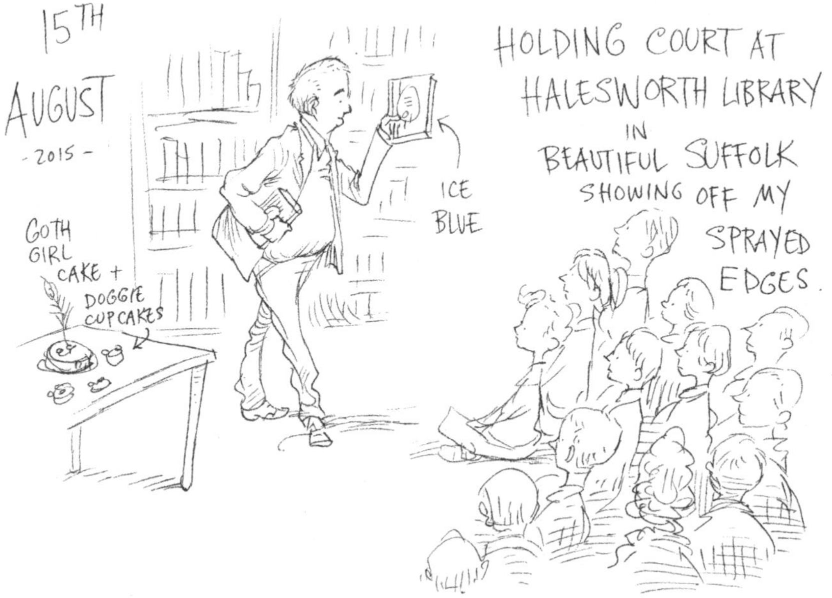
15TH AUGUST -2015-
HOLDING COURT AT HALESWORTH LIBRARY IN BEAUTIFUL SUFFOLK SHOWING OFF MY SPRAYED EDGES.
ICE BLUE
GOTH GIRL CAKE + DOGGIE CUPCAKES

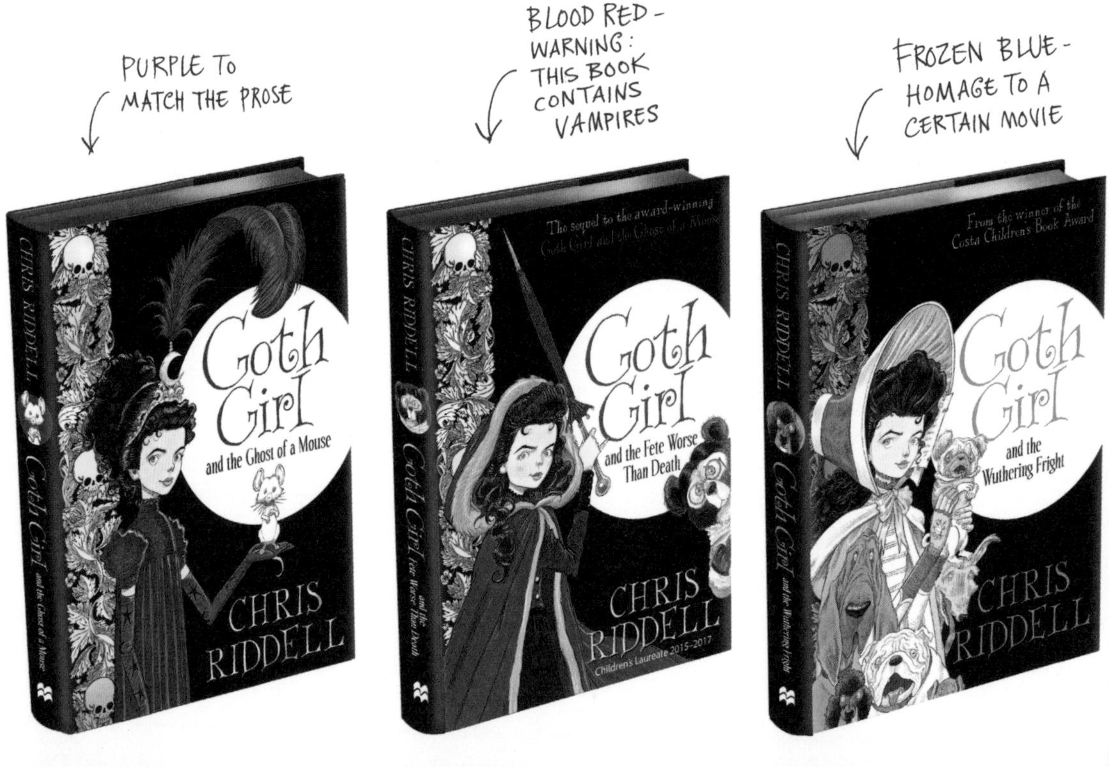
PURPLE TO MATCH THE PROSE
BLOOD RED - WARNING: THIS BOOK CONTAINS VAMPIRES
FROZEN BLUE - HOMAGE TO A CERTAIN MOVIE
Goth Girl and the Ghost of a Mouse
CHRIS RIDDELL
The sequel to the award-winning Goth Girl and the Ghost of a Mouse
Goth Girl and the Fete Worse Than Death
CHRIS RIDDELL
Children's Laureate 2015–2017
From the winner of the Costa Children's Book Award
Goth Girl and the Wuthering Fright
CHRIS RIDDELL

18TH AUGUST
- 2015 -

WHICH BROUGHT A VISIT FROM THE KINDLY SHADE OF NOSTALGIA

I FOUND A PHOTOGRAPH...

ME AND MY SON WILLIAM ↑
23 YEARS AGO...

EIGHT MILE WALK THROUGH THE NORFOLK COUNTRYSIDE...

NOW FOR A LITTLE SIT DOWN.

19TH AUGUST
- 2015 -

LISTENING TO BEETHOVEN THIS AFTERNOON

RADIO TRE

ENVELOPED IN A DAILY WORLD OF BEAUTY

WHY I LOVE THE B.B.C.

20TH AUGUST
- 2015 -

37

AUTUMN

HOME

Relaxing With Pens, Pencils and Paper

23rd AUGUST -2015-

SUNDAY SKETCHING

I DID A SERIES OF DRAWINGS EACH MORNING SITTING UP IN BED. SEE OVER THE PAGE →

THESE ARE SOME RANDOM PAGES FROM ONE OF MY SKETCHBOOKS, INCLUDING THIS DRAWING OF 'THE WATCHER ON THE ROCK' WHO BECAME MISS MACINTOSH IN 'OTTOLINE AND THE PURPLE FOX'

...And breathe

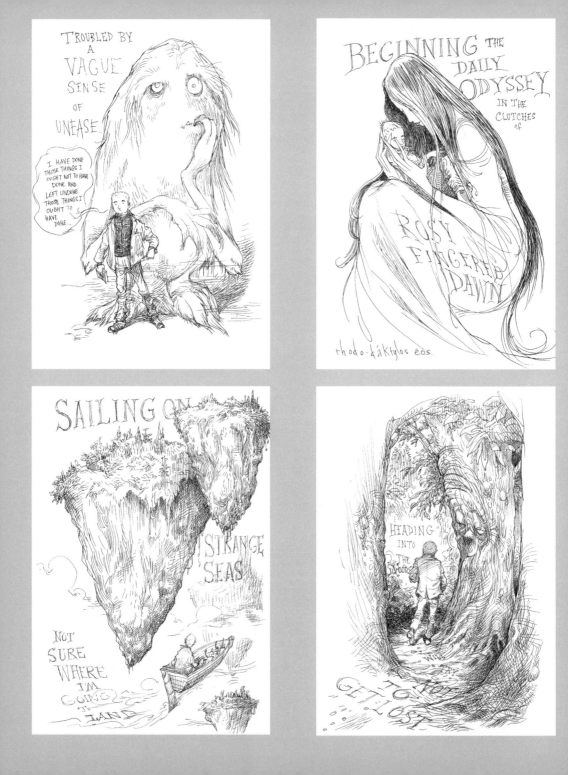

SPEND THE DAY
WITH THE
BELLE
of
AMHERST
AND A
SOFT PENCIL
DRAWING AN
EMILY DICKINSON PICTURE
BOOK.

24TH
AUGUST
- 2015 -

WILD NIGHTS - WILD NIGHTS!
WERE I WITH THEE
WILD NIGHTS SHOULD BE
OUR LUXURY!

FUTILE - THE WINDS -
TO A HEART IN PORT.
DONE WITH THE COMPASS-
DONE WITH THE CHART!

ROWING IN EDEN -
AH, THE SEA!
MIGHT I BUT MOOR - TONIGHT-
IN THEE!

EMILY
DICKINSON

THE WORLD FEELS DUSTY,
WHEN WE STOP TO DIE...
WE WANT THE DEW THEN
HONORS TASTE DRY.

FLAGS VEX A DYING FACE
BUT THE LEAST FAN
STIRRED BY A FRIEND'S HAND
COOLS LIKE THE RAIN

MINE BE THE MINISTRY
WHEN THY THIRST COMES...
DEWS OF THYSELF TO FETCH
AND HOLY BALMS

EMILY DICKINSON

HOPE
IS THE THING WITH
FEATHERS
THAT PERCHES IN THE SOUL,
AND SINGS THE TUNE
WITHOUT THE WORDS,
AND NEVER STOPS AT ALL,
AND SWEETEST IN THE GALE
IS HEARD,
AND SORE MUST BE THE
STORM
THAT COULD ABASH THE
LITTLE
BIRD
THAT KEPT SO
MANY WARM.

EMILY DICKINSON

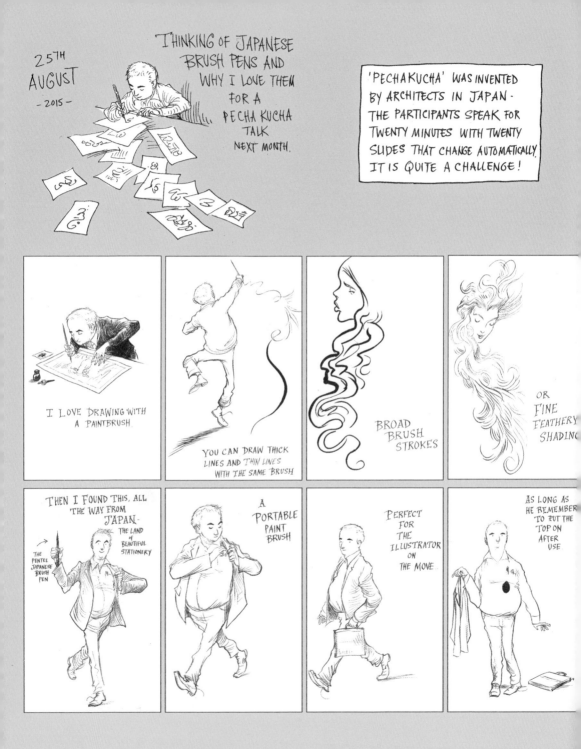

'GOODBYE AUGUST' - YOU'VE BEEN LOVELY.

SEPTEMBER

1ST SEPTEMBER
- 2015 -

IT'S A MARATHON NOT A SPRINT
IT'S A MARATHON NOT A SPRINT
IT'S A MARATHON NOT A SPRINT...

2nd September
- 2015 -

TALKING TALKING TALKING...

A GREAT BIG CUDDLE

ON THE RADIO TODAY

TIRED BUT HAPPY!

3rd SEPTEMBER
- 2015 -

'A GREAT BIG CUDDLE' - POEMS FOR THE VERY YOUNG IS A WONDERFUL BOOK BY THE POET MICHAEL ROSEN. IT CONTAINS ELEPHANTS...

47

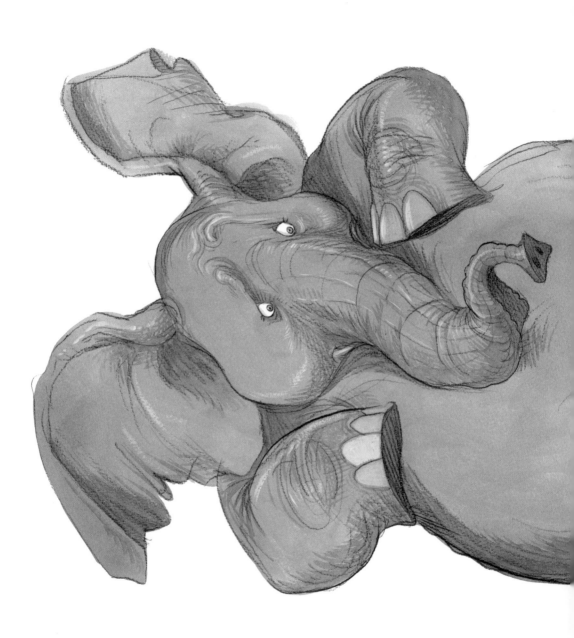

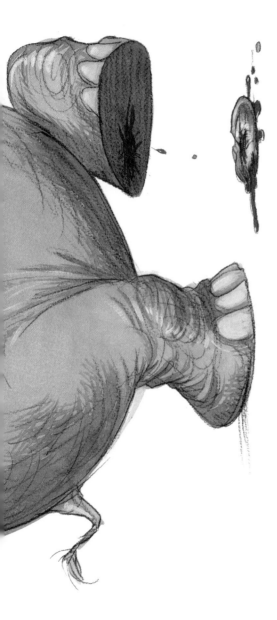

DON'T SQUASH

Don't squash your toes, Doris,
don't squash your toes.
Don't squash your nose, Doris,
don't squash your nose.

Don't squash your bun, Doris,
don't squash your bun.
Don't squash the sun, Doris,
don't squash the sun.

Don't squash cars, Doris,
don't squash cars.
Don't squash the stars, Doris,
don't squash the stars.

Don't squash the fly, Doris,
don't squash the fly.
Don't squash the sky, Doris,
don't squash the sky.

DRAWING THIS WEEK'S
CARTOON FOR THE OBSERVER
IS HEARTBREAKING

AND I'M
ANGRY...

4TH SEPTEMBER - 2015 -

14TH SEPTEMBER
-2015-

ENJOYING AN
INDIAN TAKEAWAY
IN
SUNNY
DURBAN
AT THE
END OF THREE
WONDERFUL
SCHOOL VISITS

THE SEA

MOBILE PHONE MAST

DE-BONED MUTTON ROTI

TOASTED JANINE

WINDSWEPT ANDREA

15TH
SEPTEMBER
-2015-

LITERARY
LAUNDRY

AN
OTTOMAN

HOLDING COURT
AT
'LOVE BOOKS' IN
JO'BURG AS,
WHAT MY GERMAN FRIEND HIEKE
CALLS, THE CHILDREN'S
LAUNDRETTE AFTER A WONDERFUL VISIT
TO ROEDEAN SCHOOL

FLYING BACK
TO THE UK   on billows
of
goodwill

16TH SEPTEMBER
-2015-

Thank you Pan Macmillan South Africa.

BACK
FROM
MY
TRAVELS

17TH
SEPTEMBER
-2015-   ETTING
OFF ON
NEW ADVENTURES
ON
FRIDAY NIGHT.

Drawing Jeremy
Tying himself in Knots
for The Observer

18TH
SEPTEMBER
~2015~

GOOD TO BE BACK
IN MY STUDIO

THIS DOUBLE
ACT DOMINATED
MY CARTOONS
FOR QUITE
A WHILE...

19TH SEPTEMBER —2015—

AT THE BODLEIAN LIBRARY IN OXFORD

DRAWING AT THE BIG DRAW EVENT...

HAVING A STRANGE FEELING OF

BEING WATCHED.

HUBRIS, MY METAPHORICAL MULE AND I SET OFF ON A BOOK TOUR TO PROMOTE

Goth Girl and the Wuthering Fright

WALES

20th September —2015—

THIS IS ONE OF THE MINI-BOOKS TO BE FOUND IN THE BACK OF MY GOTH GIRL BOOKS. THIS IS THE CAREER OF A MUSICAL WEREWOLF FROM 'GOTH GIRL AND THE WUTHERING FRIGHT'

HISTORY OF A HOUND

Illustrated by Sir Christopher Riddle-of-the-Sphinx RA

THE BARKER OF SEVILLE

The career of Bramble the werewolf, supernatural hound of song, began in Copenhagen, where he delighted audiences in the comic opera about a marmalade-loving spaniel.

THE CALL OF THE MILD

This was followed by a moving performance in a musical tale of shy huskies.

A MIDSUMMER NIGHT'S SCREAM.

Next Bramble toured Europe in the hit comedy about werewolves lost in the woods.

THE IMPORTANCE OF BEING HAIRY

Bramble took London by storm as Lord Ernie in a drawing-room farce about mistaken pedigree.

THE HUNDRED AND ONE ALSATIANS

Another triumph followed with Bramble's starring role in a musical spectacular about tap-dancing German shepherds.

THE MARRIAGE OF FIDO

Now a great star, Bramble the werewolf returned to Copenhagen in a sequel to *The Barker of Seville*, set in a grand kennel.

WHIMPER-RISER

Finally Bramble confirmed his place in musical history with his sensitive interpretation of a set of songs by Franz Sherbet about a wolfhound that can't get up in the morning.

NO THOUGHTS OF PIG'S HEADS AND INITIATION CEREMONIES AS I DREW ON SCHOOL LIBRARY WALLS

POO

SAVE IT FOR SUNDAY

21ST SEPTEMBER -2015-

DRAWING LIVE AT THE LAUNCH OF 'A GREAT BIG CUDDLE' WITH MICHAEL ROSEN AND LOVELY FOLKS FROM WALKER BOOKS AT THE OCTOBER GALLERY IN LONDON.

I AM ANGRY

NOT ANGRY AT ALL.

22nd SEPTEMBER -2015-

IN GLASGOW TAKING MY LITERARY DOG SHOW POODLE FOR A STROLL...

DELIGHTFUL BREEZE

CARLO THE YANKEE DOODLE POODLE

ON MY "GOTH GIRL AND THE WUTHERING FRIGHT TOUR".

23rd SEPTEMBER -2015-

I'M FLYING THROUGH THE AIR ON PUBLICATION DAY OF GOTH GIRL AND THE WUTHERING FRIGHT

24TH SEPTEMBER -2015-

ICE BLUE SPRAYED EDGES

CATAPAULTED SNOW MEN

58

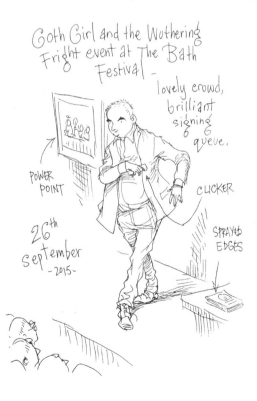

SITTING ON A METAPHORICAL
BRIGHTON BEACH PONDERING
THE FUTURE OF THE LABOUR
PARTY FOR MY
OBSERVER
CARTOON.

25TH SEPTEMBER
-2015-

Goth Girl and the Wuthering
Fright event at The Bath
Festival -

lovely crowd,
brilliant
signing
queue.

POWER
POINT

CLICKER

26th
September
-2015-

SPRAYED
EDGES

59

MET THE VERY YOUNG AND VERY CHARMING JOE SUGG YESTERDAY IN BATH.

WE TALKED ABOUT BANDERBEARS AND THE EDGE CHRONICLES

27th SEPTEMBER -2015-

28th SEPTEMBER -2015-

← THE RIBBON

CUTTING THE RIBBON TO OPEN BRUNSWICK PRIMARY SCHOOL IN HOVE

DRAWING BLIND ON SWIPE T.V. FOR RTE

EASONS

EYES SHUT

← EYES SHUT

CLAIRE THE VERY TALENTED PRESENTER

29TH SEPTEMBER -2015-

AT EASON'S BOOKSHOP IN DUBLIN

SIGNING COPIES OF "GOTH GIRL AND THE WUTHERING FRIGHT" WITH MY NEW FRIEND

ICE BLUE SPRAYED EDGES

THE EASON'S ELF

ICE BLUE SPRAYED EDGES.

30TH SEPTEMBER -2015-

Thinking About THE HUMAN RIGHTS Act

FOR AMNESTY INTERNATIONAL

2nd October

- 2015 -

WATCHING ENGLAND
CRASH OUT OF THE RUGBY
WORLD CUP

3rd October
-2015-

MUDDY FIELD
WRESTLING-
SQUASHED FOOTBALL
IN
GOTH GIRL AND
THE WUTHERING
FRIGHT.

AT THE CHELTENHAM FESTIVAL OF LITERATURE
SO NOT TOO DEPRESSED.

DRAWING ON WATERSTONES
CHELTENHAM
WALLS

(PILLAR)

AS
THE
MASKED
MAN
OF
MYSTERY

"THE
DOODLER"

4th
October
-2015-

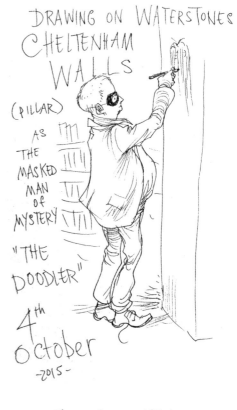

MY
GIANT
HAIRY
HAND

← JAPANESE
BRUSH PEN

← VISUALISER

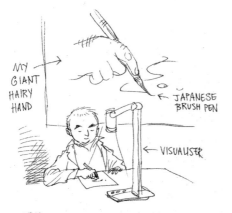

HAVING A WONDERFUL
TIME AT THE CHELTENHAM
FESTIVAL OF LITERATURE
DRAWING WITH A
VISUALISER

5TH OCTOBER
-2015-

TALKING ON STAGE AT
ROEDEAN SCHOOL
IN
BRIGHTON

6TH
OCTOBER
-2015-

SHOWING
OFF
MY MEDAL

"ROEDEAN
HAIR"
CAUSED BY
SEA
BREEZE

Packing my bag and preparing to go to the Children's Literature Festival in Sardinia tomorrow

7TH OCTOBER
-2015-

IN THE COMPANY OF PRINCESS JOANNA OF NORFOLK

VERY HAPPY LAUREATE

HAVING MY PHOTO TAKEN AT THE 10TH TUTTESTORIE FESTIVAL IN CAGLIARI
- SARDINIA -

MR MUNROE

LARGEST ZOOM LENS IN ITALY

RAYBANS

A TORRENT OF ITALIAN CHILDREN

8TH OCTOBER
-2015-

RAINED OFF and Rained on in

Cagliari at the tuttestorie festival this afternoon

9th October
-2015-

BLUE SKY

SUN SHINE

DOING A SARDINIAN SUN DANCE

10th October

AS EXTRA festival 10 tuttestorie gets back on track.

65

Feeling
the
love
at
Tuttestorie
eXtra
10
festival

.IN
THE
SARDINIAN
SUN

11th
October

THE HUNTING OF THE SNARK

Let us take them in order. The first is the taste,

    Which is meagre and hollow, but crisp:

Like a coat that is rather too tight in the waist,

    With a flavour of Will-o'-the-wisp.

Its habit of getting up late you'll agree

    That it carries too far, when I say

That it frequently breakfasts at five-o'clock tea,

    And dines on the following day.

The third is its slowness in taking a jest.

    Should you happen to venture on one,

It will sigh like a thing that is deeply distressed:

    And it always looks grave at a pun.

68

INTERVIEWING A PURPLE FOX IN MY STUDIO THIS AFTERNOON

Ottoline and the Purple Fox

21st October
— 2015 —

DEMONSTRATING THE ART OF PENCIL SHARPENING AT THE BUSINESS ACADEMY IN BEXLEY

MECHANICAL PENCIL SHARPENERS ARE THE WORK OF THE DEVIL

POSSIBLY SPELLBOUND

surgeon's scalpel

22nd October
— 2015 —

Ottoline was just about to take the lid off bin number thirty-four and put the junk inside when a furry face appeared.

37

39

MARVELLING AT A.F. HARROLD'S ABILITY TO TIP-TOE THROUGH TINY POETRY LOVERS AT OUR EVENTS IN READING

#Things You find in a Poet's Beard

26TH October -2015-

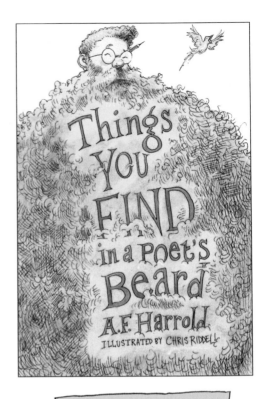

Things YOU FIND in a Poet's Beard
A.F. Harrold
ILLUSTRATED BY CHRIS RIDDELL

THIS IS ONE OF MY FAVOURITE POEMS BY THE WONDERFUL ASHLEY HARROLD

LESSER KNOWN,
BUT NOT LESS IMPORTANT

IF YOU THINK THE TOOTH FAIRY HAS IT TOUGH SPARE A THOUGHT FOR THE FINGER NAIL PIXIE WHO HAS TO COLLECT CAST OFF NAIL CLIPPINGS.

AND THEN THERE'S THE EAR WAX LEPRECHAUN WHO SCRAPES THE TOPSIDES OF PILLOWS AND THE LEFT OVER ELF WHO SCRAPES PLATES.

76

NOT FORGETTING THE POOR OLD BOGEY BOGGART
AND THE DREAD-INDUCING DANDRUFF BANSHEE
WHOSE SCREAMS FORETELL A FALL OF HAIR SNOW.

LOOKING SAD'S THE BELLY-BUTTON FLUFF GARGOYLE
WHO WAITS ON ROOFTOPS TO COLLECT DRIFTING FLUFF,
OF WHICH, UP THERE, THERE'S NEVER VERY MUCH.

AND FINALLY THERE'S THE PESKY EYEBALL SPRITE
WHO COLLECTS EYEBALLS THAT FALL OUT IN THE NIGHT.
HE CATCHES THEM IN HIS SILKY PAWS AND JUGGLES.

A.F. HARROLD

DOODLING AT THE
BOOK NOOK IN HOVE
for 'Chris Riddell's
Doodle-a-Day
Book'

27th
October
-2015-

SKETCH
BOOKS

OUR
WHO   NIP.
WHAT MUNROE
WHERE HAIRY
?   BOGPERSON
      NORWAY

DOODLING IS THE
'LITTLE BROTHER'
OF DRAWING AND
I THINK WE SHOULD
ALL DOODLE
EVERY DAY!

November 1

How to draw an ear:

① ② ③
④ ⑤ ⑥

(310)

Draw your ear here!

October 24

Give Lord Goth's guests something
to catch in their nets.

(300)   (301)

WORKING ON MY
NEXT PICTURE
BOOK

WONDERFUL
DAY IN
MY
STUDIO

28th October
-2015-

AT
The Bush
Theatre
holding an
"Ask The
Laureate"
event at
The
STORYSTOCK
festival

LAUREATE
LOGS
VOL. 1 & 2.

LOVELY AUDIENCE

29th
October
-2015-

I thought I
heard a Bander
bear's
Yodel...

EXPLORING THE
DEEP WOODS FOR
THE FINAL EDGE CHRONICLE

30th October -2015-

Perfect
Saturday
Afternoon

NEW ZEALAND
SAUVIGNON
BLANC

Sitting in the
autumnal sunshine in my
garden, looking forward to
The Rugby World Cup Final
31st October
-2015-

SPENDING THE DAY WITH ORPHEUS, Radio Three and a Pastel Pencil

BLISSFUL SUNDAY

1st NOVEMBER
- 2015 -

THIS IS A POEM BY NEIL GAIMAN THAT I HEARD ON THE RADIO AND HAD TO COPY OUT. IT IS CALLED 'ORPHEE'

ORPHEUS WAS A MUSICIAN. HE MADE SONGS. HE KNEW MYSTERIES.

ONE DAY THE PANTHER GIRLS HIGH ON WINE AND LUST CAME PAST AND TORE HIM FLESH FROM FLESH.

HIS HEAD STILL SANG AND PROPHESIED AS IT FLOATED DOWN TO THE SEA.

(DO NOT LOOK BACK.
DO NOT
  LOOK
    BACK.)

THERE WAS A GIRL, AND HE SAID
SHE WAS HIS GIRL. HE FOLLOWED
HER TO HELL WHEN SHE DIED.
YOU COULD DO THAT WHEN
  YOUR GIRLFRIEND DIES:
THERE ARE ENTRANCES TO HELL
  IN EVERY MAJOR CITY.

SO MANY DOORS,
  WHO HAS TIME TO
    LOOK BEHIND
      EACH
      ONE?

WHEN ORPHEUS WAS YOUNG
HE GOT THE GIRL BACK FROM
  HELL SAFELY.
THAT'S WHERE THE YEARS
    CAME FROM.
EURIDICE COMES HOME
FROM HELL AND THE FLOWERS
BLOOM AND THE WORLD
PUDDLES AND QUICKENS,
  AND IT'S
    SPRING.

BUT THAT
WAS NEVER
  GOOD
  ENOUGH.

AND BEFORE THAT SPRING STORY
IT WAS A LIFE AND DEATH TALE.
WE GOT A MILLION OF THEM.

IF HE HADN'T LOOKED BACK,
IF HE JUST HADN'T
  LOOKED BACK,

THEN ALL THE PEOPLE WOULD
COME BACK FROM THE DEAD
  ALL THE TIME,
  EACH OF US,
    NO MORE GHOSTS,

NO MORE DARKNESS

81

I WOULD GO TO HELL TO SEE
YOU ONCE MORE.
THERE'S A DOOR ON THE THIRD FLOOR
OF THE NEW YORK PUBLIC LIBRARY,
ON THE WAY TO THE MEN'S TOILETS,
BY THE LITTLE CHARLES ADDAMS GALLERY.
IT'S NEVER LOCKED.
YOU JUST HAVE TO OPEN IT.

I WOULD GO TO HELL
FOR YOU.

I WOULD TELL THEM STORIES
THAT ARE NOT FALSE AND
THAT ARE NOT TRUE. I WOULD
TELL THEM STORIES UNTIL THEY
WEPT SALT TEARS AND
GAVE YOU BACK TO ME
AND TO THE WORLD.

IT DOESN'T HAVE TO BE A YEAR.
I'D TAKE A DAY. I'D TAKE AN HOUR.
I'D WALK IN FRONT OF
YOU TO THE
LIGHT.

BUT I'D LOOK BACK,
WOULDN'T I.
WE ALL WOULD.

THE ONES WHO CAN'T LOOK
BACK, WHO CAN ONLY STARE
INTO THE SUNRISE
AHEAD OF THEM,
STARE INTO THE GLORIOUS
FUTURE.

THOSE PEOPLE DON'T GET TO VISIT
HELL.

SO ORPHEUS CAME BACK
AND CARRIED ON, BECAUSE
HE HAD TO, AND HE MADE MAGIC
AND SANG SONGS.
HE TAUGHT THAT THERE WAS
ONLY TRUTH IN DREAMS.
THAT WAS ONE OF THE MYSTERIES:

IN DREAMS THE VEIL WAS
LIFTED AND YOU COULD SEE SO FAR
FORWARD YOU MIGHT AS WELL
HAVE BEEN
LOOKING BACK.

SOME DIE IN WASHINGTON D.C.
OR IN LONDON OR IN MEXICO.
THEY DO NOT LOOK FORWARD TO
THEIR DEATHS. THEY GLANCE
ASIDE, OR DOWN, OR THEY
LOOK BACK.
EVERY HOUR WOUNDS.
THAT WAS WHAT SHE TOLD ME.

82

EVERY HOUR WOUNDS,
THE LAST ONE KILLS.

AND LOOKING BACK NOW,
SHE'S STANDING NAKED IN THE MOONLIGHT.
HER BREAST IS ALREADY BLACKENING,
HER BODY A FEAST OF TINY WOUNDS.
IZANAGI FOLLOWED HIS WIFE TO
THE SHADOW LANDS, BUT
HE LOOKED BACK:
HE SAW HER FACE,
HER DEAD FACE,
AND HE FLED.

I DREAMED TODAY OF
BONE-WHITE HORSES,
STAMPING AND NUZZLING IN THE
BRIGHT SUNSHINE,
AND OF ORANGE POPPIES
WHICH SWAYED AND DANCED IN
THE SPRING WIND.

(DO NOT LOOK BACK).

SHE HAD THE SOFTEST LIPS
HE SAID. HE SAID
SHE HAD THE SOFTEST LIPS
OF ALL
AND HER HEAD STILL SANG
AND PROPHESIED AS
IT FLOATED
DOWN TO
THE
SEA.

NEIL GAIMAN

CONTEMPLATING THE COMPLETE DEATHS IN SHAKESPEARE FOR

The new SPY MONKEY SHOW

2nd NOVEMBER

— 2015 —

DESDEMONA
OTHELLO

CORDELIA
KING LEAR

OPHELIA
HAMLET

THESE IMAGES WERE CREATED FOR A CARD GAME TO PROMOTE THE COMEDY SHOW 'THE COMPLETE DEATHS (OF SHAKESPEARE)' BY THE VERY FUNNY TROUPE OF CLOWNS CALLED 'SPYMONKEY'

CHIRON & DEMETRIUS
TITUS ANDRONICUS

ROMEO
ROMEO AND JULIET

JULIET
ROMEO AND JULIET

BEING GIVEN A VISION OF A BRIGHT EDUCATIONAL FUTURE AT THE UNIVERSITY of BIRMINGHAM SCHOOL

UoBS

3rd NOVEMBER
- 2015 -

RECITING THE BOOK OF COMMON PRAYER IN CONVERSATION WITH ELIZABETH LAIRD

IBBY HANS CHRISTIAN ANDERSEN PRIZE NOMINEE

Waterstones

We have erred and strayed like lost sheep...

THE REMARKABLE KLAUS FLUGGE 2

4th NOVEMBER
- 2015 -

YOU WAIT AGES FOR A LAUREATE AND THEN THREE SHOW UP AT ONCE...

LISTENING TO DAME JACQUELINE WILSON READ FROM HER TEENAGE DIARIES AT THE J.M. BARRIE AWARDS

LIFETIME ACHIEVEMENT AWARD

FRONT ROW SEAT ↓

MALORIE BLACKMAN

5TH NOVEMBER
- 2015 -

DRAWING A QUICK SPIRIT BEAR IN AID OF GREENPEACE AT THE LAUNCH OF "ISLAND" BY NICKY SINGER

Waterst

6TH NOVEMBER
- 2015 -

Button
Bop

ON STAGE AT
THE
STREAM
FESTIVAL
at
STREATHAM
&
CLAPHAM
HIGH SCHOOL

WITH THE

BIG FRIENDLY ROSEN

7TH
NOVEMBER
— 2015 —

SUNDAY WITH
NEIL GAIMAN'S
SCORPIO BOYS

And a
pastel
Pencil

8TH NOVEMBER
— 2015 —

DESK
DREAMING...

IN MY
STUDIO

9TH NOVEMBER
— 2015 —

NORFOLK
BOUND

HEAD FULL
OF IDEAS

PORTFOLIO FULL
OF
DREAMS

VERY
HAPPY

10TH NOVEMBER
— 2015 —

REMEMBERING

11th NOVEMBER

— 2015 —

AT SHIRLEY'S ILLUSTRATOR'S SALON

DOESN'T THIS MAN EVER SHUT UP?...

...SO THERE I WAS IN A CASTLE IN IRELAND HAVING DINNER WITH MCNULTY FROM 'THE WIRE'...

SHIRLEY HUGHES

ANTHONY BROWNE

JANE RAY

TED DEWAN

CLARA VULLIAMY

POSY SIMMONDS

CHARLOTTE VOAKE

12TH NOVEMBER

— 2015 —

Walking down Norfolk country lanes with Princess Joanna

13TH November

— 2015 —

NEWS FROM PARIS

REDRAWING MY OBSERVER CARTOON

14TH November

— 2015 —

TERRIBLE SHOOTINGS ON THE STREETS OF PARIS BY TERRORISTS

DOODLING A
BOOK WIZARD ON
A PILLAR
IN
WATERSTONES
PICCADILLY

IMPRESSIONABLE
child

DOODLE-
A-DAY
BOOK

16TH
NOVEMBER
- 2015 -

IN A LAUREATE CLUSTER
AT
SIR JOHN SOANE'S
MUSEUM

MALORIE
BLACKMAN

TONY
HALL

JACQUELINE
WILSON

MICHAEL
MORPURGO

for the launch of the
B.B.C. 'GET READING'
Campaign

17TH NOVEMBER
- 2015 -

FEELING AUTUMNAL

IN MY NORFOLK
STUDIO

18TH
NOVEMBER
- 2015 -

PHUT!

WRITING
IN
MY NORFOLK
STUDIO...

and waiting
for the
muse to
pay a
visit.

19th November

-2015-

90

91

Letting the Story tumble out....

Ottoline and the Purple Fox

24TH NOVEMBER -2015-

SAYING GOODBYE TO NORFOLK

FOR A WHILE

25th November -2015-

92

BALANCING THREE EVENTS IN ONE DAY -

NORFOLK CHILDREN'S BOOK CENTRE 'READING FOR PLEASURE' CONFERENCE

CAMPAIGN FOR DRAWING 15TH ANNIVERSARY CELEBRATION

NORWIC

LONDON

HOUSE OF ILLUSTRATION E.H.SHEPARD'S W.W.I WORK - TALK

26th NOVEMBER -2015-

27TH November

– 2015 –

DAVE'S COMICS

SIGNING BOOKS
and
Drawing Doodles in
one of my favourite
Book Shops
anywhere.

28TH
November
-2015-

GOTH
GIRL

SLEEPER AND THE
SPINDLE

OTTOLINE

LOOKING THROUGH MY
DAUGHTER KATY'S SKETCHBOOKS
AND
THINKING OF OLD
BLOCKS AND
CHIPS...

KATY STUDIED
ILLUSTRATION
AT MANCHESTER
SCHOOL OF ART

29TH NOVEMBER

-2015-

SAYING GOOD BYE TO MY FATHER

MORRIS RIDDELL
1934 - 2015

30TH NOVEMBER

- 2015 -

Joyful morning talking to Reception classes at DOWNS INFANTS SCHOOL

NEW LIVES

1st DECEMBER
— 2015 —

Launching "MY LITTLE BOOK OF BIG FREEDOMS" FOR AMNESTY INTERNATIONAL at the BRITISH LIBRARY

THE HUMAN RIGHTS ACT IN WORDS & PICTURES.

...for my Dad

2nd DECEMBER
— 2015 —

DRAWING 'SOMETHING ELSE' AT THE KEATS MEMORIAL LIBRARY IN HAMPSTEAD WHILE KATHRYN CAVE READS HER CLASSIC BOOK.

MY HEART ACHES AND A DROWSY NUMBNESS PAINS MY SENSE...

3rd December
— 2015 —

KATHRYN CAVE • CHRIS RIDDELL

Something Else

OVER a quarter of a MILLION copies sold!

He just wants to find somewhere to belong . . .

READING A LOVELY LETTER FROM

RUSSELL GETTING AWAY FROM IT ALL

RUSSELL BRAND AND REMEMBERING AMAZING EXPERIENCE OF WORKING TOGETHER – SENDING HIM HEARTFELT BEST WISHES.

4TH DECEMBER
– 2015 –

CONVERSING WITH THE CRIMSON VIXEN IN my studio

OTTOLINE AND THE PURPLE FOX

5TH December
– 2015 –

FIRE SIDE CONTEMPLATION

FUTURE PROJECTS

6TH December
– 2015 –

TRYING TO KEEP MY COOL AS DEBBIE FROM THE ARCHERS READS TWEEDLEDUM AND TWEEDLEDEE EXTRACT for me to illustrate at the HOUSE of ILLUSTRATION FUNDRAISER at The Camden Centre

7TH December
– 2015 –

The Beaver brought paper, portfolio, pens,

    And ink in unfailing supplies:

While strange creepy creatures came out of their dens,

    And watched them with wondering eyes.

98

NORFOLK BOUND

9TH December

— 2015 —

BLustery Day
in
Norfolk
FIRE WATCHING
10TH December

— 2015 —

CONTEMPLATING
CLIMATE CHANGE AND
THE WORLD WE'RE LEAVING
FOR
OUR
CHILDREN

for Sunday's
Observer
Cartoon

11TH December

— 2015 —

DINNER PARTY TIME

PAPER MICE
PLACE SETTINGS

12TH December

— 2015 —

99

SOFA SKETCHING
SUNDAY

Norfolk
Happiness

13TH December

- 2015 -

HERE ARE SOME PAGES
FROM THE PAPERCHASE
SKETCHBOOK

EXIT NORFOLK
IN PURSUIT OF
THE SNARK

TING-A-LING

14TH December
- 2015 -

ATTEMPTING
TO BE INSPIRATIONAL
AT THE
AWARDS CEREMONY
at
The
Business
Academy,
Bexley

YOUNG PEOPLE

OLD PERSON

15TH December
-2015-

APPRECIATING THE
WORK of THE
LAMP POST POET
IN
BIG
CITY

#Ottoline
And The
Purple Fox

16TH December
-2015-

RAINY
DAY
IN
THE
STUDIO

on a
snark
hunt

17TH December
-2015-

RUMINATING ON
THE MYSTERY OF MIDDLE-AGED
MALE
HAIR

THINNING

SPROUTING

BRISTLING

GREYING

19TH
December
—2015—

SUNDAY
DREAMING...

ADVENTURES
AHEAD

20TH December
— 2015 —

MOURNFUL DAY
READING THE LESSON AT MY
FATHER'S FUNERAL

MY
FATHER'S
TWEED →
JACKET

"FOR I HAVE
LEARNED, IN
WHATSOEVER
STATE I AM,
THEREIN TO BE
CONTENT."

21ST December
—2015—

AT HOME DOING
IMAGINARY
WORK

22nd December
— 2015 —

BOXING DAY

♯ SSSHHHH ! KEEP YOUR VOICE DOWN.

OBSERVING THE **JUB JUB**

As I continue to hunt the Snark...

27th December — 2015 —

LOSING MY CHRISTMAS BEARD, READY FOR A CLEAN SHAVEN NEW YEAR.

SNARK HUNTING BEAVER

FORK

THIMBLES

SOAP

28th December — 2015 —

Then a scream, shrill and high, rent the shuddering sky,

And they knew that some danger was near:

The Beaver turned pale to the tip of its tail,

And even the Butcher felt queer.

He thought of his childhood, left far far behind —

That blissful and innocent state —

The sound so exactly recalled to his mind

A pencil that squeaks on a slate!

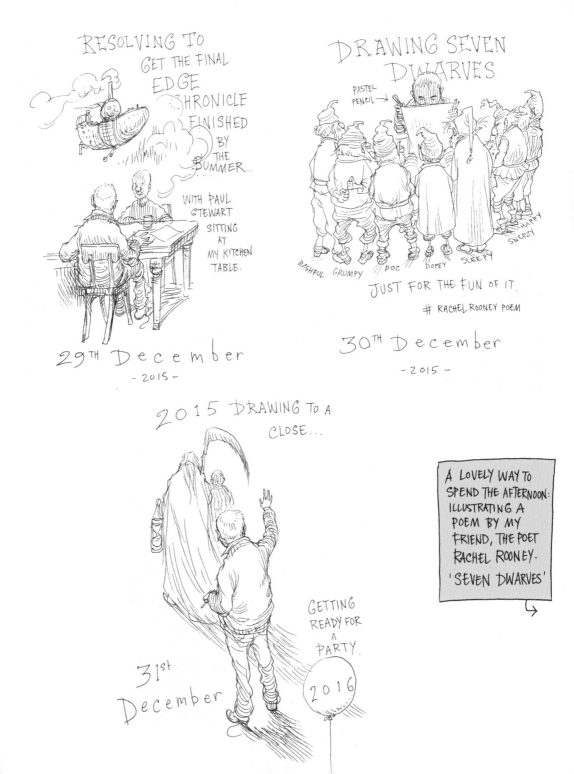

RESOLVING TO GET THE FINAL EDGE CHRONICLE FINISHED BY THE SUMMER...

WITH PAUL STEWART SITTING AT MY KITCHEN TABLE.

29TH December
- 2015 -

DRAWING SEVEN DWARVES

PASTEL PENCIL →

BASHFUL   GRUMPY   DOC   DOPEY   SLEEPY   HAPPY   SNEEZY

JUST FOR THE FUN OF IT.

RACHEL ROONEY POEM

30TH December
- 2015 -

2015 DRAWING TO A CLOSE...

GETTING READY FOR A PARTY.

2016

31ST December

A LOVELY WAY TO SPEND THE AFTERNOON: ILLUSTRATING A POEM BY MY FRIEND, THE POET RACHEL ROONEY. 'SEVEN DWARVES'

↳

SEVEN
DWARVES

ONE HAD ANGER ISSUES.
AND HE BLAMED THEM ALL ON
ME.

ONE STAYED IN HIS BEDROOM
SO WE MET INFREQUENTLY.

ONE GOT WORD-ALLERGIC
KEPT ON SNEEZING WHEN I SPOKE.

ONE WAS ALWAYS
GRINNING
YET HE COULDN'T TELL A JOKE.

ONE SEEMED KEEN. HE FLIRTED
BUT HE FAILED TO MAKE A
PASS.

ONE LOOKED CUTE (AND STUPID).

HE GOT WORSE WHEN SMOKING GRASS.

ONE BELIEVED IN HEALING
THOUGH HE NEVER WROTE
A NOTE.

NOW I'M LYING IN A GLASS BOX
WITH AN APPLE DOWN MY THROAT.

RACHEL
ROONEY

113

SPENDING THE DAY AT FAIRLIGHT PRIMARY SCHOOL IN BRIGHTON

WITH BANDERBEARS & GHOST MICE

6TH January
- 2016 -

A DAY IN MY STUDIO AT THE END OF THE GARDEN #BLISS

7TH January
- 2016 -

ATTEMPTING TO AVERT MY EYES

AS I DRAW MY OBSERVER Cartoon for Sunday

BR EXIT

8th January
- 2016 -

ON FLIGHTS OF FANCY

At the bottom of the garden

9th January
- 2016 -

114

LOUNGING ABOUT...
LAZY SUNDAY

10th January —2016—

VISITING ST. JOHN'S
COLLEGE IN KEMPTOWN BRIGHTON

MEETING WONDERFUL PUPILS WITH SPECIAL NEEDS AND SPECIAL CHARM

GUS' BEAUTIFUL DRAWING

GUS

GUS

MY DRAWING OF GUS

12TH January —2016—

HUNTING THE SNARK...

Just finished!

TING-A-LING-A-LING

11th January —2016—

REMEMBERING DAVID BOWIE'S BROTHER TERRY

WHO WAS A FRIEND OF MINE MANY YEARS AGO...

AS I ILLUSTRATE 'THE BEWLAY BROTHERS' IN TRIBUTE TO DAVID.

13TH January —2016—

115

WORLD OF
MY OWN

SUSSEX
COUNTRY
SIDE

SKETCHBOOK

PENCIL
CASE

MUSIC AND INSTAGRAM

TRAIN JOURNEY
SKETCHING
TIME TRAVEL

14TH January
-2016-

I DREW THESE WHILE
LISTENING TO THE ALBUM
'SEVEN SWANS' BY
SUFJAN STEVENS

THE DRESS LOOKS NICE
ON YOU
Sufjan Stevens.

ALL THE TREES OF THE FIELD
WILL CLAP THEIR HANDS
Sufjan Stevens.

CASIMIR PULASKI DAY

Sufjan Stevens.

SEVEN SWANS

Sufjan Stevens.

A GOOD MAN IS HARD TO FIND

Sufjan Stevens.

IN THE DEVIL'S TERRITORY

Sufjan Stevens.

WE WON'T NEED LEGS TO STAND

Sufjan Stevens.

A SIZE TOO SMALL

Sufjan Stevens.

SISTER

Sufjan Stevens.

DRAWING PICTURES AT THE
SOUTHERN SCHOOLS BOOK AWARDS
CONGRATULATIONS TO
BALI RAI and
"Web of Darkness"
2015
WINNER

ROEDEAN SCHOOL

2nd
Shortlisted authors

ALAN GIBBONS
"HATE"
SARA CROWE
"BONE JACK"
KEREN DAVID
"SALVAGE"
JAMES/JUNO DAWSON
"SAY HER NAME"

15TH January —2016—

DRAWING
THE
ROMANOVS
for
The
Literary
Review

PETER
THE
GREAT

PAUL
THE
REALLY
NOT
VERY
GREAT
AT
ALL.

16TH January
—2016—

TEA WITH EMILY
GRAVETT

SNOW outside

Redbush
Tea

Fantastic
sketch
books

ROARING
FIRE

Talking about
Picture Books.

17th January —2016—

ATTENDING A VIGIL AT
ST. ANDREWS CHURCH IN THE CITY OF LONDON
FOR REFUGEE WELCOME
CAMPAIGN

18th
January
—20-16-

AT THE POETRY CAFÉ
IN
LONDON
LOOKING AT NEW
WORK FROM FOYLE
YOUNG POET AWARDS.

ROBYN
FROM
BOOK
TRUST

RUTH
FROM
THE
POETRY
SOCIETY

19th January - 2016-

INTERVIEWING THE BRILLIANT
JIM KAY ABOUT HIS ILLUSTRATED
HARRY POTTER

IN
THE CRYPT
BELOW
THE GUILDHALL

IN
THE
CITY OF
LONDON

20th January
—2016-

THIRTEEN

THE BOYS HAVE FOOTBALL AND SKATE RAMPS.
THEY CAN RIDE BMX AND PLAY BASKETBALL IN THE COURTS BY THE FLATS UNTIL MIDNIGHT.

THE GIRLS HAVE SHAME.

ONE DAY,
WHEN WE ARE GROWN AND WE HAVE MINDS OF OUR OWN,
WE WILL BE KIND WOMEN, WITH NICE SMILES AND FAMILIES AND JOBS.

AND WE WILL SIT,
WITH THE WEIGHT OF OUR LIVES AND OUR PAIN

PUSHING OUR BODIES DOWN INTO THE BUS SEATS,

AND WE WILL SEE THIRTEEN-YEAR-OLD GIRLS FOR WHAT WILL SEEM LIKE THE FIRST TIME SINCE WE'VE BEEN THEM,

AND THEY WILL BE SITTING IN FRONT OF US, LAUGHING

INTO THEIR HANDS AT OUR SHOES OR OUR JACKETS,

AND ROLLING THEIR EYES AT EACH OTHER.

WHILE OUT OF THE WINDOW,
IN THE SUNSHINE,
THE BOYS WILL BE CHEERING EACH OTHER ON,

AND DARING EACH OTHER TO JUMP HIGHER AND HIGHER.

KATE TEMPEST

I LOVE THIS POEM BY KATE TEMPEST AND ILLUSTRATED IT WHILE SITTING ON A TRAIN ON MY WAY BACK FROM LONDON

Splashing through puddles in the winter sunshine with Princess Joanna of Norfolk

23rd January -2016-

DRAWING THE DEATHS IN SHAKESPEARE for SPY MONKEY Theatre production...

FLY FROM TITUS ANDRONICUS

PASTEL PENCIL

24th January -2016-

IN MY VERY TIDY NORFOLK STUDIO.

CAN I DOODLE ABOUT THIS IN MY LAUREATE LOG?

NO.

25TH January -2016-

TOP SECRET MEETING IN VERY SMALL OFFICE # SSSHHHHH !...

HAVING LUNCH WITH OUR GREATEST LIVING CARTOONIST

(OR ONE OF THEM!)

(QUENTIN BLAKE RAYMOND BRIGGS RALPH STEADMAN GERALD SCARFE...)

POSY SIMMONDS

SKETCHBOOK HEAVEN

26TH January -2016-

THESE ARE FROM AN ILLUSTRATED EDITION
OF NEIL'S EXTRAORDINARY NOVEL SET IN A
HIDDEN WORLD BELOW THE STREETS OF LONDON

NEVERWHERE

Neil Gaiman

ILLUSTRATED BY CHRIS RIDDELL

Saturday afternoon stroll through the kingdom with Princess Joanna of Norfolk

30th January
-2016-

Returning to Brighton Re-invigorated and full of plans of which I cannot speak...

31st January YETI.
-2016-

DRAWING FOR A VERY DISCRIMINATING AUDIENCE AT

BEAUTIFUL SCHOOL LIBRARY

Katy

Dana

Arran

scarlet

patrick

Yuki

THE CHILDREN'S LAUNDRETTE

CAULDWELL SCHOOL

2nd February
-2016-

RISQUE 19th HIKING SKIRT

SENSIBLE SUIT

MY OWN LONG SUFFERING WIFE.

WATCHING RALPH FIENNES IN IBSEN'S "THE MASTER BUILDER" AT THE OLD VIC

3rd February -2016-

Happy National Library Day!

Day!

celebrating at the Jubilee Library BRIGHTON

6th February

– 2016 –

THE SIMPLEST WAY TO MAKE SURE THAT WE RAISE LITERATE CHILDREN IS...

TO SHOW THEM THAT READING IS A PLEASURABLE ACTIVITY. AND THAT MEANS.

FINDING BOOKS THAT THEY ENJOY, GIVING THEM ACCESS TO THOSE BOOKS, AND LETTING THEM READ THEM.

NEIL GAIMAN.

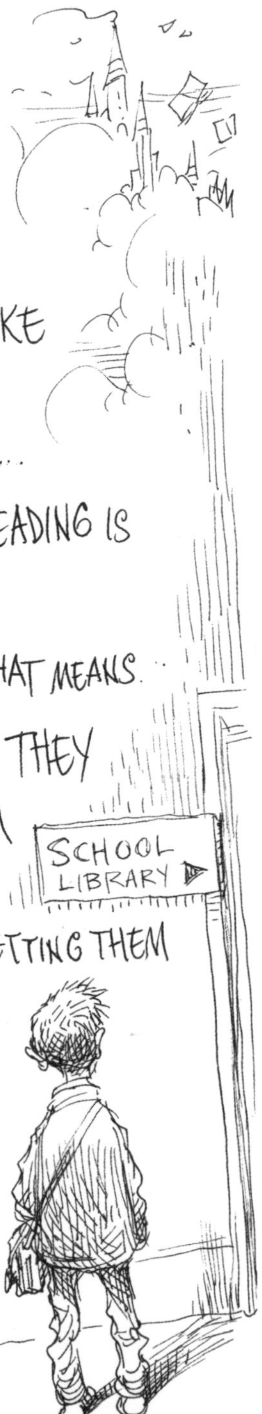

SCHOOL LIBRARY

LISTENING TO
SIR DEREK
JACOBI
AT THE MUSEUM
OF LONDON

GREAT VOICE

LGBT
CONFERENCE

READING A PICTURE
BOOK ABOUT TWO
MALE PENGUINS WHO
RAISED A CHICK AT NEW
YORK ZOO   #HEARTWARMING

7TH February
- 2016 -

Sitting at my kitchen table
with poet Rachel Rooney
discussing
plans...

YOU SHOULD
DRAW SOME
GIRLS WITH
SHORT HAIR...

THAT COULD
BE
POETIC...

8th February
- 2016 -

My editor
Hannah visiting
to talk
picture books...

I BUMPED
MY HEAD
ON THE
LUGGAGE
RACK ON
THE TRAIN
HERE.

WORK IN
DEVELOPMENT

TALLEST
EDITOR
IN
CHILDREN'S
PUBLISHING

9TH February
- 2016 -

Pontificating at
Varndean sixth form college

MY WIFE
WASHED
MY JEANS.
I DIDN'T
ASK HER
TO...

10TH February
- 2016 -

129

THIS IS AN EXTRACT FROM NEIL'S POEM 'THE SCORPIO BOYS IN THE CITY OF LUX' WHICH I FIRST DREW IN A SKETCHBOOK IN SARDINIA

OH, THEY STARE, THE SCORPIO BOYS,

IT'S AN ACT OF MAGIC OF COURSE. IF YOU BELIEVE IN THEM AT ALL

IF YOU SEE THEM YOU'LL BE LUCKY.

SO DAMN LUCKY

BEATEN UP AND LEFT FOR DEAD BY THE PILTDOWN MEN SINGING

"WE ARE WE ARE THE PILTDOWN MEN WE ARE WE ARE"

THEY STUMBLE DOWN THE ROADS OF THE CITIES OF TWILIGHT BREAKING BOTTLES AND PUKING IN GUTTERS,

SOMEONE FINDS YOU AND PICKS YOU UP AND CARRIES YOU

HOME.

MAYBE IT WAS US.

YOU NEVER KNOW.

A cigarette traces a shape in the air, Something made out of light and SMOKE.

SO YOU KNOW IT'S MAGICAL SOMEONE SAYS IT'S LUCKY AND WHO KNOWS WHAT WILL HAPPEN? STRANGER THINGS HAPPEN IN CITIES.

EVEN SMALL CITIES.

TAKE LUX, FOR EXAMPLE:

A CITY THAT ISN'T EVEN
THERE

LIKE ALL CITIES: IT IS A MAGICAL
DESCRIPTION,
A WAY OF MAKING IMPOSSIBLE
THINGS HAPPEN
AT A
DISTANCE.

LIKE A POEM OR
A WHISPER

OR A SAUCER FILLED WITH INK -

YOU CAN STARE INTO IT,
OR DIP YOUR PEN.

EITHER WAY IT WILL TAKE YOU TO
INVISIBLE PLACES,

OPEN A DOOR IN YOUR HEARTS
TO US,

SHARP-NOSED AND SHABBY GENTEEL
WITH INK-SPOTS AND CINDER-BURNS
ON OUR CLOTHES.

WHEN THERE ARE ENOUGH OF US,
WE WILL BECOME

A
CITY.

DOING IT BECAUSE
WE BELIEVE IN IT.
BECAUSE THE STORIES NEED
TO BE DESCRIBED
AND COME TO US FOR THEIR

FACES.

NEIL GAIMAN

THE GREAT ESCAPE

NOW, IN THE QUIET OF THE STUDIO AT THE BOTTOM OF THE GARDEN,
I REMIND MYSELF OF THE UNFORGIVING CHURCH PEWS,
MY FATHER'S ENDLESS SERMONS AND THE WINE GUMS
BESTOWED ON ME BY MRS. STOCK
      LIKE A BENEDICTION.

OF THE HOT TEARS DAMMING BEHIND MY EYES
ON THAT FIRST DAY OF SCHOOL
WHEN MY MOTHER LET GO OF MY HAND
AND HOW, AN HOUR LATER, HEAD BELOW THE TABLE TOP,
I SECRETLY WEPT.

OF THE STEWED PRUNES SMUGGLED
OUT FROM UNDER THE VIGILANCE OF THE DINNER LADIES
IN THE POCKETS OF MY TROUSERS
AND DROPPED SECRETLY INTO THE FLOWER BEDS
AS, LIKE A PRISONER OF STALAG LUFT,
I PLANNED MY ESCAPE.

CHRIS
RIDDELL

Laureate planning meeting

Catherine the Great
Philippa the incomparable
Ian the ebullient
Sarah the walker wizard
The Children's Launderette.
Robyn the poets' champion
Claire the event conqueror

15th February
- 2016 -

Talking about reading for pleasure and School libraries on RADIO FOUR 'YOU & YOURS'...

and enjoying Winifred Robinson's laugh.

16th February
- 2016 -

Channelling Mad king Ludwig of Bavaria

at Schloss BLUTENBERG

I'll put him in my next Goth Girl book...

and the International Youth Library

#library heaven

17th February
- 2016 -

Returning from Munich completely unchanged.

SCHLOSS RIDDELL

18th February
- 2016 -

134

Drawing the bags beneath David Cameron's eyes for The Observer

"They're getting bigger..."

19th February
—2016—

At my friend Heike Roesel's private View At The Round Georges in Brighton *

"It's the children's launderette"

Beautiful etchings — "Hundertwasser meets Klee"

* 14-15 Sutherland Road BN2 0EQ

20th February
—2016—

THE ROYAL BOX

AT THE ROYAL FESTIVAL HALL

Drawing James Campbell's very funny 'Comedy for Kids' Show live at The Imagine Festival

21st February
—2016—

Back in Big City With a small hairy friend of mine...

Ottoline and the Purple Fox.

22nd February
—2016—

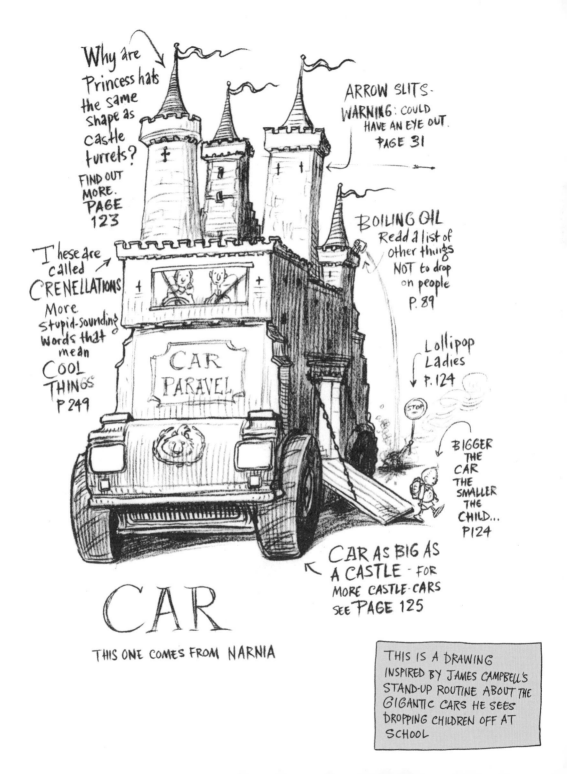

Why are Princess hats the same shape as castle turrets? FIND OUT MORE. PAGE 123

ARROW SLITS. WARNING: COULD HAVE AN EYE OUT. PAGE 31

These are called CRENELLATIONS More stupid-sounding words that mean COOL THINGS P 249

BOILING OIL Read a list of other things NOT to drop on people P. 89

CAR PARAVEL

Lollipop Ladies P.124

BIGGER THE CAR THE SMALLER THE CHILD... P124

STOP

CAR AS BIG AS A CASTLE - FOR MORE CASTLE-CARS SEE PAGE 125

CAR

THIS ONE COMES FROM NARNIA

THIS IS A DRAWING INSPIRED BY JAMES CAMPBELL'S STAND-UP ROUTINE ABOUT THE GIGANTIC CARS HE SEES DROPPING CHILDREN OFF AT SCHOOL

Visiting my next door neighbour to work on The Edge Chronicles

PAUL STEWART'S HOUSE

23rd February -2016-

MEETING TO WORKOUT DETAILS OF BRIGHTON FESTIVAL ARTS EVENT...

HOME IS WHERE THE HEAD IS...

DRAWING & PHOTOGRAPHY

24th February -2016-

Home IS where the Heart IS...

DRAW SOMEONE, SOMETHING OR SOME PLACE THAT REMINDS YOU OF HOME AND THEN WEAR YOUR DRAWING OVER YOUR HEART AND HAVE A PORTRAIT PHOTOGRAPH TAKEN.

CHRIS RIDDELL

DOODLE MOUSE LIVES IN MY STUDIO AT THE BOTTOM OF MY GARDEN IN BRIGHTON.

DOODLE MOUSE

CHRIS RIDDELL -2016-

Drawing on the School Library Wall of Hertford's Juniors in BRIGHTON

RUNNING COMMENTARY

25TH February - 2016 -

Fireside chat with Charlotte from The Bookseller

Do you ever sleep?

laureate logs

26TH February - 2016 -

Reading "A GREAT BIG CUDDLE" at my local Church Hall in aid of Team Kenya

The Inscrutability of the very young

fund raising for Education in Kenya.

27th February - 2016 -

SUNDAY IN BIG CITY

Ottoline and the Purple Fox

FLOATING ON CURRENTS OF CREATIVITY

28TH February - 2016 -

Skyping at Midnight
with International
School in
Brunei

Sounds like tropical rain...

With a wavering connection...

29th February
— 2016 —

Drawing Ishmael
Whiskers for the
Booklovers at NEWTON PREP.
in Battersea

Call me Ishmael

1st March
— 2016 —

— IN PRESTON —
At The Biggest Book Show
on Earth talking about
where Books take you...

Narnia when I was eight...

2nd March
— 2016 —

On Blue Peter
Book Awards show
being presented with a Gold Blue Peter Badge

SO PROUD

The Witch from Narnia

3rd March — 2016 —

140

WHY I CAN'T LIVE WITHOUT BOOKS

SKETCH BOOK

NOSE STUCK IN A BOOK

Chris Riddell.

BOOKS ARE LIKE DOORS. YOU CAN OPEN THEM AND STEP INTO ANOTHER PLACE... OR TIME... OR WORLD

WOOF!

I MISREAD "ASLAN" IN MY HEAD AND THOUGHT, FOR A LONG TIME, HE WAS NAMED AFTER A TYPE OF DOG.

BOOKS ARE WHERE I'VE MET SOME OF MY CLOSEST FRIENDS... LIKE ALSATIAN THE LION.

FLAT STANLEY WAS SQUASHED PAPER THIN BY A FALLING BULLETIN BOARD SO DECIDED TO POST HIMSELF TO VISIT A FRIEND.

Ottoline Brown
APARTMENT 243,
The Pepperpot Bld,
3rd street,
BIG CITY 3001.

BOOKS CHANGE HOW I SEE THE WORLD - EVERYTIME I POST A LETTER I THINK OF MY FAVOURITE BOOK.

BOOKS DON'T NEED BATTERIES OR RECHARGING AND ARE READY WHEN YOU ARE.

BOOKS TAKE ME TO FARAWAY LANDS LIKE EARTHSEA ... AND THE EDGE.

BOOKS TAKE ME BACK IN TIME...

I SPEND MY TIME DRAWING AND WRITING IN BOOKS - SKETCHBOOKS. I HAVE HUNDREDS OF THEM AND I DRAW IN THEM EVERY DAY.

LIBRARIANS I HAVE LOVED

PETER AND JANE 2ᶜ

MY JOURNEY BEGINS...

I WAS DETERMINED TO CONQUER THE MOUNTAINOUS TASK OF LEARNING TO READ AIDED BY THE LADYBIRD SHERPAS, PETER AND JANE, WHO DIDN'T SEEM TO DO VERY MUCH.

THE UNEXPECTED BOOK

ONE DAY, WHILE STRUGGLING WITH PETER AND JANE, I DISCOVERED ONE OF THEIR LATER ADVENTURES. THEY DIDN'T DO VERY MUCH BUT IN EXCITINGLY LONG AND COMPLEX SENTENCES. IF ONLY I COULD REACH SUCH HEIGHTS, I THOUGHT, THEN I WOULD HAVE CONQUERED READING. THEN, IN THE LIBRARY, I PICKED UP A BOOK...

THE LIBERATION OF INCOMPREHENSION

"A GATON SAX AND THE JEWEL THIEVES" WAS FAR BEYOND MY READING ABILITIES BUT I DIDN'T MIND. IT WAS FUN, IT HAD PICTURES, IT HAD A STORY WHERE THINGS SEEMED TO HAPPEN I DIDN'T UNDERSTAND MOST OF IT BUT I LOVED IT. I WANTED MORE BOOKS LIKE THIS. THE LIBRARY BECKONED...

STORY TIME

LIBRARIANS TOOK ME IN. THEY GAVE ME STORIES. I DISCOVERED MIRKWOOD AND CLIMBED AN OAK TREE WITH BILBO BAGGINS AND SAW AN ARMADA OF BLACK BUTTERFLIES FLUTTERING ABOVE THE TREE TOPS. I WENT IN SEARCH OF MORE.

THE GATE KEEPER

MY SCHOOL LIBRARY WAS GUARDED BY A HEROIC FIGURE WHO
PROTECTED THE PEACEFUL SANCTUARY WITH AN IMPLACCABLE WILL.
THE LIBRARY WAS MY HAVEN FROM THE TURMOIL OF THE SCHOOL
DAY. THE SCHOOL LIBRARIAN WAS MY GUARDIAN.

EYES ON THE PRIZE

HER GLAMOUROUS COLLEAGUE WAS MY MUSE. MISS BARNES HELD
A SHORT STORY COMPETITION. I WON A PRIZE FOR A SCIENCE FICTION
STORY INSPIRED BY RAY BRADBURY'S "THE ILLUSTRATED MAN". I'LL
NEVER FORGET IT.

VARIS LODD

THE LIBRARIAN KNIGHTS
OF THE SECOND AGE OF FLIGHT

IN 'THE EDGE CHRONICLES' PAUL STEWART AND I MADE LIBRARIANS
OUR HEROES. VARIS LODD IS THEIR HEROIC LEADER, PREPARED TO
PUT HER LIFE ON THE LINE TO DEFEND THE GREAT LIBRARY.

COULSDON LIBRARY

THE BOOK I COULDN'T STACK

AS A SIXTH FORM STUDENT, I FOUND THE BEST SATURDAY JOB
IN THE WORLD. I WAS ADMITTED INTO THE FABLED WORLD OF
LIBRARIES. I WAS ALLOWED TO DATE STAMP BOOKS, COLLECT LATE
FEES AND TO STACK THE BOOK SHELVES. IT WAS MAGICAL.
ONE DAY, WHILE SHELF STACKING, A BOOK CAUGHT MY EYE. THE
LIBRARIANS HAD TAUGHT ME WELL. I PICKED THE BOOK UP AND READ IT.
THE NOVEL WAS "GORMENGHAST" BY MERVYN PEAKE. I'LL NEVER
FORGET IT.

Talking at the Bloomsbury ★ Sales Conference

GOOD SHOT...

7th March
- 2016 -

Chatting with the sparkling Eoin Colfer the Irish Children's Laureate on the radio.

8th March
- 2016 -

A Work day

in the studio at the bottom of the garden.

9th March
- 2016 -

BEING FILMED IN MY STUDIO AND INTERVIEWED BY KALI ON HER 10TH BIRTHDAY FOR THE BRIGHTON FESTIVAL HOUSE PROJECT

HOME IS WHERE THE HEART IS

OVER FLOWING WASTEPAPER BASKET

11TH MARCH - 2016 -

SWINGING LOW IN A
SWEET CHARIOT
Watching
muddy Field wrestling
squashed
Football

12th MARCH
- 2016 -

SUNDAY
SKETCHING IN
THE SPRING
SUNSHINE

HEAVEN

13TH MARCH
- 2016 -

POETRY, PICTURE
BOOKS,
ASK THE
LAUREATE
ART
WORKSHOPS
&
SHAKESPEARE...

CHATTING
TO THE
BRIGHTON
ARGUS
ABOUT
MY
BRIGHTON
FESTIVAL
EVENTS
IN
MAY...

14th
March
- 2016 -

NICKY COX MBE
TOUCHING MY KNEE AS I INTERVIEWED
HER AT THE LAUNCH OF THE
FIRST NEWS ihub AP...

Sitting
on
very
high
stools

15TH March
- 2016 -

147

SHAMELESSLY FLAUNTING MY GOLD BLUE PETER BADGE AT WALTHAM HOLY CROSS PRIMARY SCHOOL THIS MORNING...

THE WHITE WITCH FROM NARNIA GAVE IT TO ME...

16TH March -2016-

WAVING MY ARMS ABOUT AND COLLIDING WITH BAUBLES AS I SPEAK AT

BUT!

THE WATERSTONES BOOK PRIZE

17th March -2016-

STUDIO TIME...

WORKING AS FAST AS I CAN!

18th March -2016-

Walking on air As England win a Grand Slam

in muddy field wrestling squashed football

19th March -2016-

148

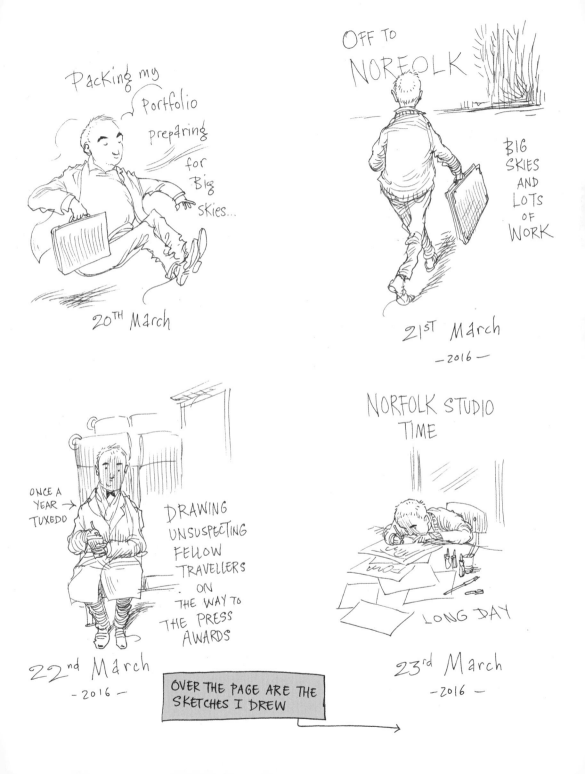

Packing my Portfolio preparing for Big Skies...

20TH March

OFF TO NORFOLK

BIG SKIES AND LOTS OF WORK

21ST March
— 2016 —

ONCE A YEAR TUXEDO →

DRAWING UNSUSPECTING FELLOW TRAVELLERS ON THE WAY TO THE PRESS AWARDS

22nd March
— 2016 —

NORFOLK STUDIO TIME

LONG DAY

23rd March
— 2016 —

OVER THE PAGE ARE THE SKETCHES I DREW

PEOPLE ON THE TRAIN

HIDING OUT WITH OTTOLINE AND MR. MUNROE IN

BIG CITY

26TH March
- 2016 -

THIS IS MY FAVOURITE SPREAD FROM 'OTTOLINE AND THE PURPLE FOX'

As they peeped out from the mailbox they saw a herd of miniature zebra trot along 5th Street and cross the road.

Happy Easter

SUNDAY
IN
THE
COUNTRY

March
27th

-2016-

Working as storm Katie
blows herself out

March 28th -2016-

Off in a world of my own...

#Ottoline And the purple Fox

29th March -2016-

Hard at work as deadline looms...

TICK TICK
TICK
TICK

30th March -2016-

Last day in Norfolk for a while...

31st March -2016-

155

AT THE BOLOGNA BOOK FAIR

DRAWING A POTATO AT THE "ACHTUNG KARTOFFEL!"

SUPERMARKET OF DESIRE

EXHIBIT

TWO GERMAN DESIGNERS IN WHITE COATS

CURIOUS ITALIAN CHILD

GOODBYE MR. CHIPS

HOW DID I GET HERE?

2nd APRIL
-2016-

PROMENADING THROUGH BOLOGNA ON A SUNNY SUNDAY AFTERNOON

PUBLICITY WARRIOR PRINCESS CATHERINE

3rd APRIL
-2016-

SMALL INTIMATE DINNER FOR 76 HOSTED BY MY FRIENDS AT MACMILLAN

THE SPIRIT OF BOLOGNA BOOK FAIR

SURROUNDED BY CO-EDITION GOODWILL

4th APRIL
-2016-

157

RETURNING TO THE NEWLY FASHIONABLE SEASIDE RESORT OF BRIGHTON

VERY HAPPY

5th APRIL -2016-

Watching Timothy Spall's brilliant performance in 'The Caretaker' at the Old Vic

6th April -2016-

TIMOTHY SPALL SENT ME THIS SKETCH WHICH HE DREW OF HIS CHARACTER IN REHEARSALS OF 'THE CARETAKER' BY HAROLD PINTER. IT IS ON MY STUDIO WALL

Back in the Studio Working on Ottoline...

7th April -2016-

We're all in this together except for those that are not...

PANAMA PAPERS

8th APRIL
- 2016 -

MY DAEMON, ISHMAEL.

AMIDST THOSE DREAMING SPIRES AT THE OXFORD LITERATURE FESTIVAL

9th APRIL
- 2016 -

SUNDAY MORNING CONVERSATION WITH MR. FICKLING THE BOOK WIZARD OF OXFORD

WAND

HIS DARK MATERIAL

10th APRIL
- 2016 -

BEING HAUNTED BY A LOOMING DEADLINE

I'M GETTING THERE..

OTTOLINE AND THE PURPLE FOX

11th APRIL
- 2016 -

LOST IN LONDON

I THINK I'VE GOT THE WRONG DAY...

BRICK LANE

THURSDAY NOT TUESDAY

12TH APRIL —2016—

I GROW OLD, I GROW OLD AND I SHALL WEAR THE BOTTOMS OF MY TROUSERS ROLLED ?...

54 TODAY.

13TH APRIL —2016—

I LOVE THIS QUOTE FROM 'THE LOVE SONG OF J. ALFRED PRUFROCK'

160

I SHOULD HAVE BEEN A PAIR OF

RAGGED
CLAWS

SCUTTLING ACROSS THE FLOORS

OF SILENT SEAS.

T.S. ELIOT

AT THE SKETCHBOOK SOCIAL WHERE
#LONDON BOOK & SCREEN WEEK

THE VERY TALENTED WILL GRILL DREW ME A PASTEL GIRAFFE.

14TH APRIL
— 2016 —

KEEPING MY HEAD ABOVE PAPER...

JUST.

#Ottoline and the Purple Fox

16TH APRIL
— 2016 —

Taking a moment in my sunny garden...

THEN BACK INTO THE STUDIO TILL LATE

17TH APRIL
— 2016 —

DRAWING IS MEDITATION

BEEN MEDITATING A LOT LATELY...

19TH APRIL
— 2016 —

THIS IS A SKETCH FROM THE PAPERCHASE SKETCHBOOK

162

HAVING LUNCH WITH
THE GREAT ROGER MCGOUGH
AND HIS EDITOR MARY
MAKING POETRY
— PLANS —
20th APRIL —2016—

SUMMER WITH
MONIKA

ROGER MCGOUGH

ILLUSTRATED BY
CHRIS RIDDELL

WORKING LATE

21st APRIL
-2016-

DRAWING
BORIS
THE
BREXIT
LION
for
the
Observer

22nd
APRIL
-2016-

APPROACHING THE END OF A LONG JOURNEY WITH MY GOOD FRIENDS, Ottoline & Mr. Munroe.

23rd APRIL -2016-

INK BLOT FROM PEN AFFECTED BY CABIN PRESSURE!

EXCALIBUR WAS MELTED DOWN TO MAKE MY LAUREATE MEDAL...

BEAUTIFUL BOOK - 'IMAGINARY FRED' ILLUSTRATED BY OLIVER JEFFERS

25TH APRIL -2016-

IN CONVERSATION WITH EOIN COLFER AT QUEENS UNIVERSITY BELFAST

FINISHING Ottoline and the Purple FOX!

24th APRIL -2016-

DRAWING ANSWERS TO QUESTIONS IN COOKSTOWN, NORTHERN IRELAND

UNICORN... DON'T ASK.

26TH APRIL -2016-

WANDERING
TOWARDS
STORMONT

#PALPABLE
SENSE OF
HISTORY

TO TALK
TO
LOVELY
LIBRARIANS
AND
PUPILS
WITH

BOOK
TRUST

NORTHERN
IRELAND

27TH
APRIL
—2016—

A
BRILLIANT,
MOVING AND
INVIGORATING
FEW
DAYS.

HOME

FEELS WONDERFUL!
28th April

167

FORGET ABOUT THE PAST AND TAKE MY ADVICE, BREXIT...

DRAWING AN UNREPENTANT MURDOCH for my OBSERVER CARTOON 29th April —2016—

MY HOUSE IS OPEN TO ART LOVERS...

TEA & CAKE IN THE GARDEN

ART INSIDE

MY STUDIO ←

30th APRIL —2016—

169

THE MINISTER FOR EXAMS

WHEN I WAS A CHILD I SAT AN EXAM.
THE TEST WAS SO SIMPLE
THERE WAS NO WAY I COULD FAIL.

QUESTION ONE. DESCRIBE THE TASTE OF THE MOON.

IT TASTES LIKE CREATION I WROTE,
IT HAS THE FLAVOUR OF STARLIGHT.

QUESTION TWO. WHAT COLOUR IS LOVE?

LOVE IS THE COLOUR OF THE WATER A MAN
LOST IN THE DESERT... FINDS, I WROTE.

QUESTION THREE. WHY DO SNOWFLAKES MELT?

I WROTE, THEY MELT BECAUSE THEY FALL
ON TO THE WARM TONGUE
OF GOD.

THERE WERE OTHER QUESTIONS.
THEY WERE SIMPLE.

I DESCRIBED THE GRIEF OF ADAM
WHEN HE WAS EXPELLED FROM EDEN.
I WROTE DOWN THE EXACT WEIGHT OF
AN ELEPHANT'S
DREAM

YET TODAY, MANY YEARS LATER,
FOR MY LIVING I SWEEP THE STREETS
OR CLEAN OUT THE TOILETS OF THE FAT
HOTELS.

WHY? BECAUSE CONSTANTLY
I FAILED
MY EXAMS.

WHY? WELL, LET ME SET A TEST.

QUESTION ONE. HOW LARGE IS A CHILD'S
IMAGINATION?

QUESTION TWO.

HOW SHALLOW IS THE SOUL OF THE
MINISTER FOR EXAMS?

BRIAN
PATTEN

AT THE 150TH
ANNIVERSARY OF THE
LONDON LIBRARY
DINNER IN A
TENT IN ST. JAMES' SQUARE
#HOB NOBBING

SARAH
ARMSTRONG-JONES
LOOKING LIKE A
YOUNGER VERSION OF
HER
AUNT.

JUST
SHAKEN
TOM
STOPPARD'S
HAND

INEZ THE
TENTH
LIBRARIAN

← Fascinating
book on Victorian
Cycling by the
Pushkin Press

4th
May
-2016-

Judging the Klaus
Flügge
Picture
Book
Prize

and

reaquainting
myself with
the joy
of
Picture
Books

5th May
- 2016

OFF TO LONDON
TO CELEBRATE MICHAEL
ROSEN'S
70TH
BIRTHDAY

PURSUED BY
A FRONTED
ADVERBIAL

- 6th May 2016-

SEE PAGE 176

OPEN
HOUSE
⟹

ENJOYING TIME OUT IN
THE GARDEN BETWEEN BOUTS
OF 'NEVERWHERE' ILLUSTRATING
7TH May -2016 -

172

173

DRAWING SATs Beasties

12th May
-2016-

and extolling the benefits of dedicated school librarians instead of pointless tests

SEE PAGES 176-177

OFF TO WATCH SPY MONKEY PERFORM THE COMPLETE DEATHS IN SHAKESPEARE AT THE THEATRE ROYAL BRIGHTON

I'VE LEFT YOU MY SECOND BEST BED...

13th May
-2016-

WITH PRINCESS JOANNA of NORFOLK (ONE OF THE MERRY WIVES OF THETFORD)

IN A BRIGHTON FESTIVAL VORTEX

AT JUBILEE LIBRARY ILLUSTRATING 'HOME IS WHERE THE HEART IS' INSTALLATION, CHILDREN'S POETRY FOR 'RAP & RHYME'...

THEN "ASK THE LAUREATE" EVENT AT THE UNIVERSITY OF BRIGHTON

14th May
-2016-

I LOVE BRIGHTON FESTIVAL GOERS.

THE LANGUAGE OF CAT

"POEMS & PICTURES"

LOVELY EVENT AT THE BRIGHTON FESTIVAL WITH RACHEL ROONEY THE POET AT THE UNIVERSITY OF BRIGHTON

15th May
-2016-

175

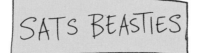

SATS BEASTIES

THE GRAPHEME

THE PHONEME

THE MORPHOLOGY CHANGING INFLECTION

THE NON-FINITE CLAUSE

THE TRIGRAPH

THE FRONTED ADVERBIAL

THE
SUBORDINATE
CLAUSE

THE
CO-ORDINATING
CONJUNCTION

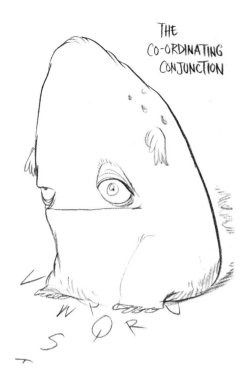

THE
AUXILIARY
VERB

THE SPLIT DIGRAPH

THE
COHESIVE
DEVICE

AFTER GOYA

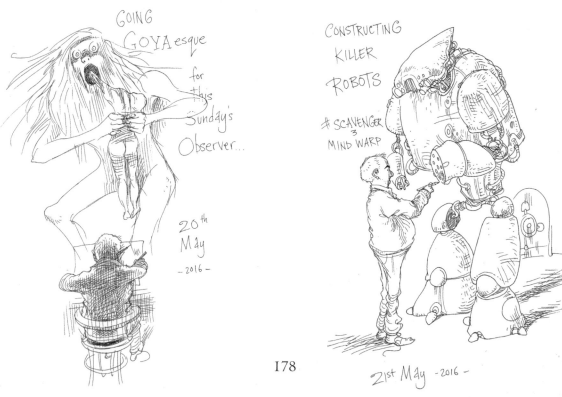

GOING GOYAesque for this Sunday's Observer...

20th May -2016-

CONSTRUCTING KILLER ROBOTS

#SCAVENGER 3 MIND WARP

178

21st May -2016-

181

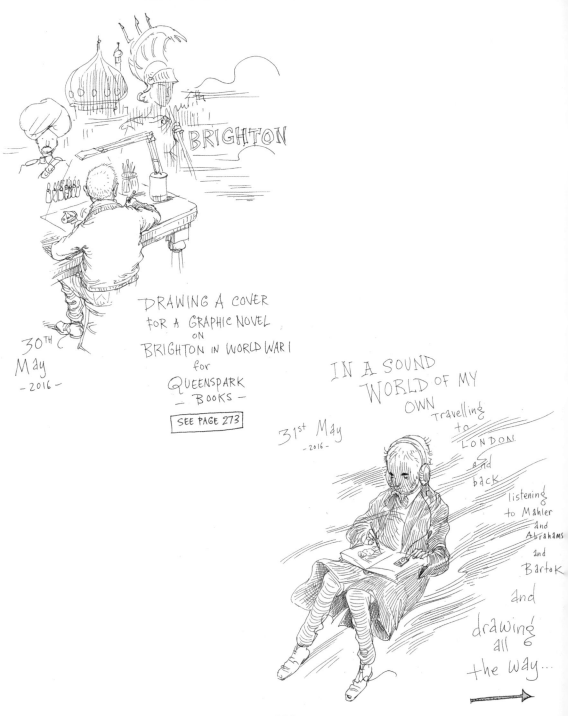

BRIGHTON

DRAWING A COVER
FOR A GRAPHIC NOVEL
ON
BRIGHTON IN WORLD WAR I
for
QUEENSPARK
— BOOKS —

SEE PAGE 273

30TH
May
-2016-

31st May
-2016-

IN A SOUND
WORLD OF MY
OWN Travelling
to
LONDON
and
back
listening
to Mahler
and
Abrahams
and
Bartok

and

drawing
all
the way...

SYMPHONY OF SORROWFUL
SONGS
GÓRECKI

BRUCH SYMPHONY N°3 OP.51
— SCHERZO —

FANTASIA ON A THEME
— BY THOMAS TALLIS —
VAUGHAN WILLIAMS

BRUCH SYMPHONY N°3 OP.51
— ADAGIO —

FESTINA LENTE
ARVO PÄRT

CANTUS IN MEMORIAM
— BENJAMIN BRITTEN —
ARVO PÄRT

Flaming
June

here so
soon...

1st
June
—2016—

187

My Anniversary!
one year of laureating today

9th June -2016-

IT HARDLY WEIGHS A THING...

CHILDREN'S LAUREATE

Thank you for All your support!

At Manchester School of Art looking at my daughter's work...

KATY RIDDELL

FIT TO BURST.

and lots of very talented students' work

#fantastic Degree Show

10th June - 2016 -

Returning from Manchester on my metaphorical Mule

11th June -2016-

HUBER'S

Meeting lots of brilliant students from Cleveland College of Art, Hartlepool

ALAN, Tom, Lauren, Rebecca, Jack, Beth, Aaron, Mikki and lots more!

in Brick Lane at their London Exhibition

joyful afternoon of drawing.

12th June -2016-

189

The BFG.
Quentin Blake

CHRIS RIDDELL

HATE DOESN'T HAVE
A CREED, RACE OR RELIGION,
IT IS POISONOUS.

BRENDAN
COX

Head in my hands at yesterday's horrific Murder of Jo Cox MP

RIDDELL
19.6.16

17th June
- 2016 -

Drawing a cartoon for The Observer

FINDING IT HARD TO CONCENTRATE
ON THE COVER OF THE LITERARY REVIEW
AS ENGLAND
DEMOLISH AUSTRALIA
AT MUDDY FIELD · WRESTLING SQUASHED
FOOTBALL

A.E. HOUSMAN

YES!

18th June
— 2016 —

MEETING WILLIAM HOGARTH AT
THE NATIONAL PORTRAIT
GALLERY

HOW DO YOU
DO?

#Sunday
gallery
sketching

19th June
— 2016 —

LIBRARIANS ARE BRIDGE BUILDERS.
THEY USE THE BOOKS OF THE PAST TO
INSPIRE THE BOOK CREATORS OF THE
FUTURE. WHEN
WE CLOSE DOWN
A LIBRARY, WE
DESTROY
THOSE
BRIDGES.

HAPPY &
HUMBLED...

20TH
JUNE
— 2016 —

CARNEGIE
GREENAWAY
PRIZE
— 2016 —

BILLOWS OF
KIND THOUGHTS

CONDUCTING AN
"ASK THE LAUREATE"
EVENT AT THE
UNIVERSITY OF EAST
ANGLIA
IN
NORWICH

MY FAVOURITE
CARTOON
CHARACTER?
DAVID
CAMERON...

← STACK OF
QUESTIONS

21ST JUNE
— 2016 —

W.G. GRACE

↑
POST IMPRESSIONIST BEARD

I WONDER, BY MY TROTH,
WHAT THOU AND I
DID, TILL WE LOVED? WERE WE
NOT WEANED TILL THEN?
BUT SUCKED ON COUNTRY PLEASURES,
CHILDISHLY?
OR SNORTED WE IN THE SEVEN SLEEPERS
DEN?
'TWAS SO; BUT THIS, ALL PLEASURES
FANCIES BE.
IF EVER ANY BEAUTY I DID SEE,
WHICH I DESIRED, AND GOT,
'TWAS BUT A DREAM OF THEE.

THE GOOD-MORROW

JOHN DONNE

WILLIAM WILBERFORCE

EXPRESSIVE EYE BROWS..

GEORGE CRUIKSHANK

crazy signature

EDWARD III

HE'S ACTUALLY GOOD...

AMERICAN ACCENT →

IN HIS PYJAMAS

WILLIAM HOGARTH

AYUBA SULEIMAN DIALLO

EMILY

ANNE

CHARLOTTE

THE BRONTË SISTERS

ON MY WAY TO MANCHESTER ON HUBRIS, MY METAPHORICAL MULE AFTER DRINKS AND CANAPES WITH THE NATIONAL LITERACY TRUST IN LONDON...

NEXT STOP THE BREAKFAST T.V. SOFA.

22nd JUNE - 2016 -

SHOWING OFF OUR MEDALS ON THE BREAKFAST T.V. SOFA WITH SARAH CROSSAN AUTHOR OF THE ASTONISHING VERSE NOVEL "ONE"

← CARNEGIE
GREENAWAY

↑ CAMERA 6.

FEELING LIBRARIAN LOVE

23rd JUNE - 2016 -

MY REACTION TO THE E.U. REFERENDUM RESULT

WHAT ABOUT OUR CHILDREN?

I DON'T WANT TO LEAVE

24th JUNE - 2016 -

A HEAVY HEART EASED BY THE ENLIGHTENED FOLK AT THE NATIONAL ASSOCIATION OF TEACHING ENGLISH CONFERENCE IN

THE CHILDREN'S LAUNDERETTE

CATHARTIC! SKETCHBOOK DOODLING.

STRATFORD UPON AVON

THESE ARE PAGES FROM THAT SKETCHBOOK →

25TH JUNE - 2016 -

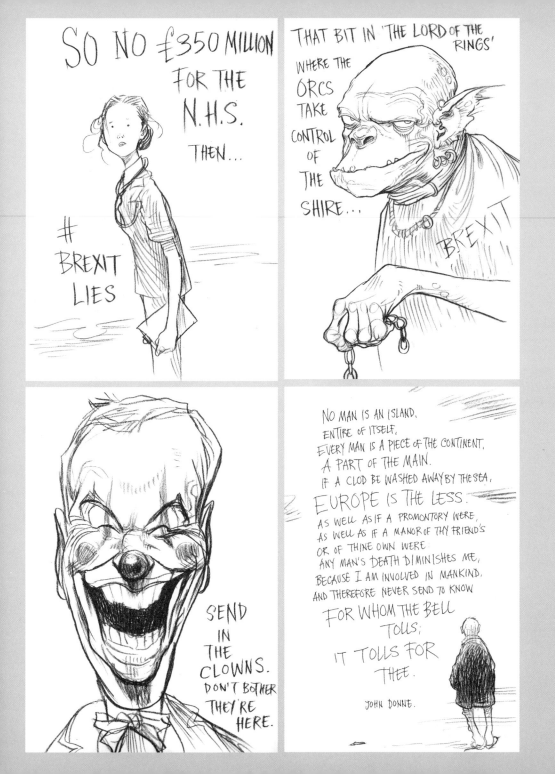

It was the closest kingdom to the queen's, as the crow flies, but not even the crows flew it. The high mountain range that served as the border between the two kingdoms discouraged crows as much as it discouraged people, and it was considered unpassable.

More than one enterprising merchant, on each side of the mountains, had commissioned folk to hunt for the mountain pass that would, if it were there, have made a rich man or woman of anyone who controlled it. The silks of Dorimar could have been in Kanselaire in weeks, in months, not years. But there was no such pass to be found, and so, although the two kingdoms shared a common border, nobody crossed from one kingdom to the next.

Even the dwarfs, who were tough, and hardy, and composed of magic as much as of flesh and blood, could not go over the mountain range.

This was not a problem for the dwarfs. They did not go over the mountain range. They went under it.

Three dwarfs, travelling as swiftly as one through the dark paths beneath the mountains:

"Hurry! Hurry!" said the dwarf at the rear. "We have to buy her the finest silken cloth in Dorimar. If we do not hurry, perhaps it will be sold, and we will be forced to buy her the second finest cloth."

"We know! We know!" said the dwarf at the front. "And we shall buy her a case to carry it back in, so it will remain perfectly clean and untouched by dust."

The dwarf in the middle said nothing. He was holding his stone tightly, not dropping it or losing it, and was concentrating on nothing else but this. The stone was a ruby, rough-hewn from the rock and the size of a hen's egg. It was worth a kingdom when cut and set, and would be easily exchanged for the finest silks of Dorimar.

It would not have occurred to the dwarfs to give the young queen anything they had dug themselves from beneath the earth. That would have been too easy, too routine. It's the distance that makes a gift magical, so the dwarfs believed.

 he drawbridge across the moat was down,
and they crossed it, although everything
seemed to be pushing them away. They could
not enter the castle, however: thick thorns filled the
gateway, and fresh growth was covered with roses.

The queen saw the remains of men in the thorns:
skeletons in armour and skeletons unarmoured. Some
of the skeletons were high on the sides of the castle,
and the queen wondered if they had climbed up,
seeking an entry, and died there, or if they had died
on the ground, and been carried upwards as the roses
grew.

She came to no conclusions. Either way was
possible.

And then her world was warm and comfortable,
and she became certain that closing her eyes for only
a handful of moments would not be harmful. Who
would mind?

"Help me," croaked the queen.

The dwarf with the brown beard pulled a thorn
from the rose bush nearest to him, and jabbed it hard
into the queen's thumb, and pulled it out again. A
drop of deep blood dripped on to the flagstones of
the gateway.

"Ow!" said the queen. And then, "Thank you!"

They walked to the
east,
all four of them, away
from the sunset and
the lands they knew,
and
into
the
Night.

Drawing a portrait for the refurbished
Discover Story Centre in Stratford,
East London

IN MY
NORFOLK
STUDIO.

'Mack
Botty
III'

EMPEROR
SMACKBOTTY
III

TINY TYRANT
FROM THE PLANET
'WAY-PAST-YOUR-BEDTIME'.

29th JUNE
- 2016 -

Back in Brighton
Spending the afternoon
Colouring

the
Deaths
in
Shakespeare
Cards

for a
new
edition.

CROSS
GARTERED

30TH JUNE
- 2016 -

REMEMBERING

1ST JULY

1916 — 2016

HUNTING THE
SNARK at
The Book
Nook
in
HOVE

2nd
July
—2016—

Lewis Carroll's
classic Nonsense
Poem...
(with a feminist
subtext)

The Hunting of the Snark...

Looking forward to hearing my dulcet tones
choosing essential classics on Radio
Three tomorrow
at 10 a.m.

...Can't
remember
what I
actually
said!

3rd
July
—2016—

Losing myself in a
metaphorical forest
as I write my new
picture book...

SHOULD HAVE
BROUGHT BREADCRUMBS...

4th
July
—2016—

EVERYTHING
IN THE
GARDEN
IS
LOVELY...

Wish I
could believe
the same
about the
country.

BREXIT
BLUES.

5th July
—2016—

203

Standing in for the B.F.G. at the launch of this year's SUMMER READING CHALLENGE

WHIZZ POPPING SNOZCUMBERS!

14th JULY
—2016—

Relaxing in my metaphorical Hammock of Happiness
16th July
—2016—

Live drawing... At the British Library Shakespeare evening as a rude mechanical
15th JULY
—2016—

HE'S BOTTOMED OUT...

A MIDSUMMER NIGHT'S DEAM

KING LEEK

THE MAIMING OF THE SHREW

ILLUSTRATING Omar Khayyam for The Literary Review...

17th JULY
—2016—

" A BOOK OF VERSES UNDERNEATH THE BOUGH
A FLASK OF WINE, A LOAF OF BREAD AND THOU
BESIDE ME SINGING IN THE WILDERNESS
AND WILDERNESS IS PARADISE NOW."

206

207

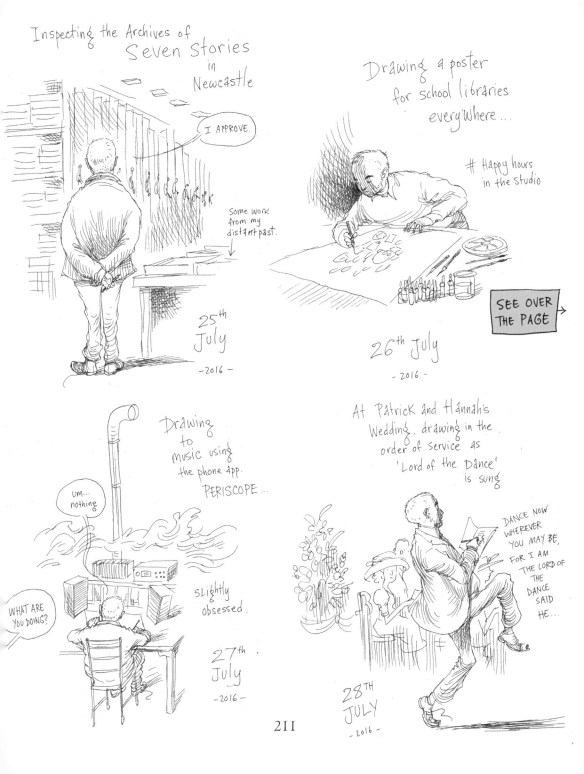

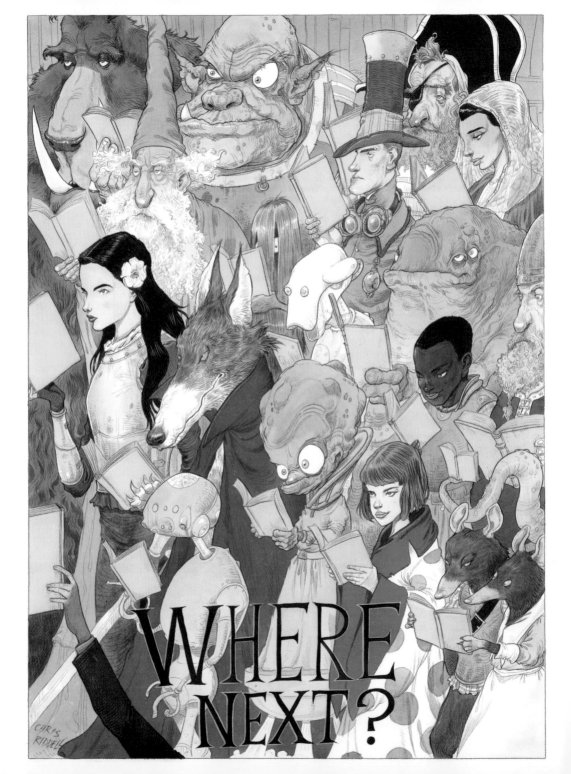

To die, to sleep,
To Sleep, Perchance to Dream; Aye, there's the rub,
For in that sleep of death, WHAT DREAMS
MAY COME,
WHEN WE HAVE SHUFFLED OFF THIS MORTAL COIL,
Must give us pause...

But that the dread of something after death,
THE UNDISCOVERED COUNTRY, from whose
bourn
No Traveller returns, Puzzles the will,
And makes us rather bear those ills we have,
Than fly to others that we know not of.
THUS CONSCIENCE DOES MAKE
COWARDS of us all...

HAMLET.

William
Shakespeare.

↑ PAUL STEWART HOLDING THE ROPE

ON AN EPIC JOURNEY TO DISCOVER WHAT LIES AT THE BOTTOM OF THE EDGE CLIFF.

2nd AUGUST -2016-

Head in the clouds in a good way...

3rd August -2016-

Hanging out with old friends from the Edge lands...

4th August -2016-

Looking out of the garden room at Princess Joanna surveying the flower meadow while listening to Vaughan Williams' Norfolk Rhapsody

5th August -2016-

216

a month in the country

6th August
-2016-
Enjoying my
Wild Flower Meadow
with the Muse Sauvignon Blanc

DRIFTING ON A Sunday Stream of Thought

writing reveries

7th August
-2016-

Travelling through imaginary grasslands on fantastical creatures.

8th August
-2016-

Drawing a creeping Lie Tree

9th August
-2016-

217

Travelling to the great floating city on the edge of the world...

10th August –2016–

on a gothic adventure with Faith Sunderly

11th August –2016–

THESE ARE CONTÉ PASTEL PENCIL ILLUSTRATIONS FOR 'THE LIE TREE' BY FRANCES HARDINGE

19th Century Hair

JOHN SINGER SARGENT

DEGAS

CLOSE HELMET
FITZWILLIAM.

JOHN
EVERETT
MILLAIS

GALLERY GOER
FITZWILLIAM

GALLERY GOER
FITZWILLIAM

THESE ARE SKETCHES I DREW
AS I WALKED THROUGH THE
FITZWILLIAM MUSEUM IN CAMBRIDGE

Popped into Macmillan Children's Books and was handed the first copy of "Ottoline And The Purple Fox"...

I'M AN URBANE FOX

Looking forward to getting out and about to talk about it, this September.

18th August - 2016 -

Decorating pages of a wonderful novel 19th August - 2016 -

I THINK I MIGHT HAVE MENTIONED 'THE LIE TREE'

Drawing live on Periscope to Music on YouTube...

then posting on Instagram facebook and Twitter

20th August - 2016 -

21st August -2016-

Drawing a Bookworme for Waterstones

224

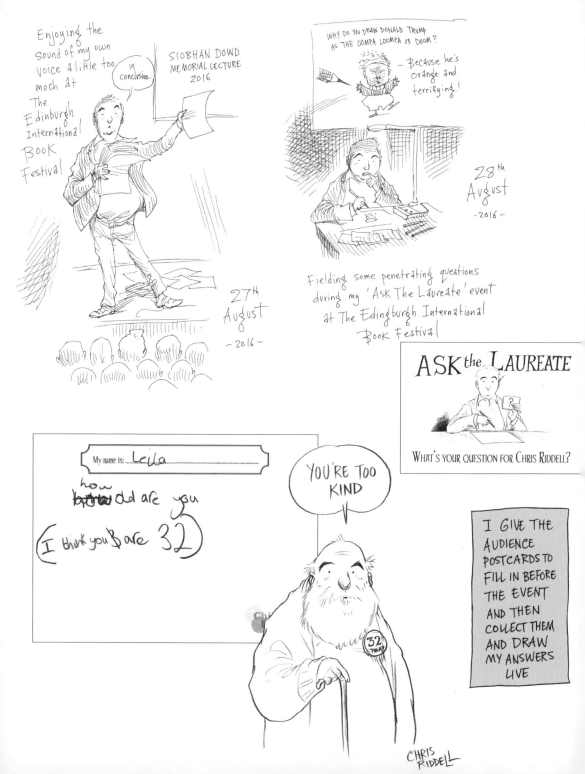

My name is: Tania

Can you draw your most embarassing moment?

ON THE SPUR OF THE MOMENT, BORROWING READING GLASSES TO READ 'MEMOIRS OF A MOUSE'. THE TINY BOOK INSIDE 'GOTH GIRL AND THE GHOST OF A MOUSE' AT THE CAPE TOWN BOOK FESTIVAL

CHRIS RIDDELL

My name is: penny

age 5

wot dog do you have

dp you have a pig

I HAVE AN INVISIBLE DOG. I DO NOT HAVE A PIG... YET.

Woof!

CHRIS RIDDELL

My name is: WHATS YOUR FAVE CHEESE?!

COS I REALLY WANNA KNOW.!!

229

I LIKE CHESHIRE CHEESE JUST BEFORE BEDTIME...

CHRIS RIDDELL

230

celebrating the publication of "Odd And The Frost Giants" at Bloomsbury's Offices in LONDON

IT's A STORY of courage, beauty and a son's love for his mother...

WARM FEELING

N 31st August - 2016 -

OVER THE PAGE ARE THE ENDPAPERS FROM 'ODD AND THE FROST GIANTS'

231

234

237

Paul Stewart
and I have
reached the half way
point in "The
Descenders"
and we want to find
out what happens
next...

7th September
- 2016 -

Drawing the back of another
sketcher's head for my
social media takeover at The
House of Illustration in
King's Cross.

GRASS
Terraces
beside the
canal at
Granary Square

8th September
- 2016 -

HELLO AGAIN, MR. CHIPS

GRAMMAR SCHOOLS

NO, WE DON'T WANT THE REST OF YOU - YOU'RE FAILURES. YOU CAN GO TO THOSE OTHER SCHOOLS WHICH WE'LL PRETEND AREN'T SECONDARY MODERNS...

THE THERESA MAY "SOCIAL MOBILITY" ACADEMY

TIRED OLD THINKING FROM A GOVERNMENT DESPERATE TO DEFLECT ATTENTION FROM ITS

GRAMMAR SCHOOLS

BREXIT FIASCO

Drawing my Cartoon for The Observer 9th September -2016-

239

WHAT BIG HANDS YOU HAVE.

The Young Adult corner

Periscope

Scottish Friendly Children's Book Tour

Drawing on the walls in four corners of Waterstones in Glasgow and filming on my phone as I draw

10th September -2016-

Drawing with a visualiser and answering 'ASK THE LAUREATE' questions

MAKING IT UP AS I GO ALONG.

AT HILLHEAD LIBRARY GLASGOW

ASK THE LAUREATE POSTCARDS IN A BOX WITH FAIRYLIGHTS

on the Scottish Friendly Children's Book Tour.

11th September
-2016-

THE CHILDREN'S LAUNDERETTE ON TOUR IN East Renfrewshire

#scottish Friendly children's Book Tour

Beth and Tom

from the Scottish Book Trust

Metaphorical laundry

12th September
-2016-

Drawing a dragon in silver pen on a black door in Waterstones Stirling

#Scottish Friendly Children's Book Tour

13th September
-2016-

scattering books across Scotland with Beth and Tom

PERTH

DECORATED BOOK BUS - "THE SARAH MAC"!

on the Scottish Friendly Children's Book Tour

ASK THE LAUREATE

14th September
-2016-

Lovely afternoon at the
Steyning Bookshop talking
about
"Odd and the Frost Giants"

Sunday in the
Studio

BLISS

STE...NG BOOKSHOP

17th
September
-2016-

18th September
-2016-

Talking about
The Edge Chronicles
with
Paul Stewart

IT'S
CHANGED,
YOU KNOW...

TELL ME
ABOUT IT...

19th September
-2016-

At the Forward Poetry Prizes
at
the Royal Festival
Hall
with the
Poet
Rachel Rooney

listening
to
extraordinary
Poetry

20th September
-2016-

Watching a
brilliantly
balletic
performance
by
Freya
Mavor in
'Good Canary'
at
The Rose Theatre
Kingston

-awing
in the
dark...

21st September
-2016-

Raising a glass to my
Wonderful publishers
Pan Macmillan

Thank you
for a splendid
launch
party

on
the publication
day
of
"Ottoline And
The
Purple Fox"

↖ MY
daughter
Katy.

22nd September
-2016-

243

BRITAIN IS BOOMING, THE BREXITEERS ARE JUBILANT, EVERYTHING WILL BE FINE!...

AS LONG AS WE DON'T ACTUALLY DO ANYTHING.

RIDDELL 25-9-16

Considering those crowing Brexiteers for my Observer Cartoon.

23rd September
- 2016 -

ENTERTAINING MY READERS WITH WITTY BANTER AT MY BOOK SIGNING at Waterstones

...and it's got a purple fox in it.

#Ottoline And The Purple Fox.

24th September
- 2016 -

Finding my way through the woods as I write my new picture book...

SUNDAY
IN
NORFOLK

25th September
-2016-

On stage in Norwich showing old family photographs...

I'm the good looking one in the bowtie...

← Power Point Slide

Stubble

Pastel Pencil

CLICKER

visualiser

Ottoline and the Purple Fox

at Avenue Junior School

And then at Norwich High School for Girls

26th September
-2016-

Speaking off the cuff - closing remarks at The Bookseller Conference at the Barbican

visual notes

READING FOR PLEASURE

READING FOR LIFE.

27th September
-2016-

245

Live drawing on the
Lauren Laverne Show and periscoping
the results

6 MUSIC

28th September — 2016 —

WORDS ARE DEAD

INTO MY ARMS

AGNES OBEL

NICK CAVE & THE BAD SEEDS

FINAL DAY

YOUNG MARBLE GIANTS

CHRIS RIDDELL

Drawing on the wall of
the 'Riddell Café' at the
Centre for Literacy in Primary
Education...

then reading
aloud to teachers
at
"going home
time"

29th
September
-2016-

READING ALOUD
IS PROBABLY THE MOST IMPORTANT THING
THAT TEACHERS CAN DO
AND NEEDS TO BE A
FREQUENT AND REGULAR
PART OF EACH SCHOOL DAY.

- CLPE -

THE CENTRE FOR LITERACY
IN PRIMARY EDUCATION.

CHRIS RIDDELL

READING ALOUD
SLOWS WRITTEN LANGUAGE DOWN
AND
ENABLES CHILDREN TO HEAR AND
TAKE IN TUNES AND PATTERNS.
IT ENABLES CHILDREN TO EXPERIENCE
AND ENJOY STORIES THAT
THEY MIGHT NOT OTHERWISE MEET.

- CLPE -

THE CENTRE FOR LITERACY
IN PRIMARY EDUCATION.

CHRIS RIDDELL

BY READING WELL-CHOSEN
BOOKS ALOUD,
TEACHERS HELP CLASSES TO BECOME
COMMUNITIES OF READERS.

ENSURING THAT THEY CAN SHARE IN
EXPERIENCES OF A WIDE REPERTOIRE
OF BOOKS THEY ENJOY
AND GET TO KNOW WELL.

- CLPE -

THE CENTRE FOR LITERACY
IN PRIMARY EDUCATION.

CHRIS RIDDELL

Drawing by lamplight and
Periscope at The Leisure Society
gig at St. Pancras
Old Church

30th
September
—2016—

FIGHT
FOR
EVERYONE

WE
WERE
WASTED

GOD HAS
TAKEN A
VACATION

YAHWEH

THE FINE
ART
OF
HANGING
ON

On stage at the 'Y' Theatre opening the "EVERYBODY'S READING FESTIVAL" IN LEICESTER WITH MY "ASK THE LAUREATE" event...

THE WALKER BEAR

THE LORD LIEUTENANT OF SURREY

telling the story of how I got trapped on a double decker bus with the Duchess of Cornwall...

1st October -2016-

My name is: JANA

I WAS UNDER SOME PRESSURE WHEN I WAS WRITING MY FIRST Q. SO, HERE IS MY SECOND ATTEMPT:

BASED ON MY NAME, HOW WOULD YOU DRAW ME?

THANK YOU

JANA - NO PRESSURE!

CHRIS RIDDELL

ASK the LAUREATE

WHAT'S YOUR QUESTION FOR CHRIS RIDDELL?

My name is: Atlanta

are you mad, bad and dangerous to know? gnomes?

THAT CHILDREN'S LAUREATE IS A MENACE!

CHRIS RIDDELL

My name is: Jessica

How did you feel when you won the Kate Greenway medal for the first time?

...LIKE THIS

SWELLING

TINGLING

GREENAWAY MEDAL

FLOATING

CHRIS RIDDELL

249

Sunday
drawing in bed

#very
happy

2nd
October
- 2016 -

Sitting up in bed drawing
and Periscoping and
then taking the drawing
to the copy shop
and getting a
hundred copies made

"The Apprentice"

Then selling them all
by four o'clock.

3rd October
- 2016 -

250

THE APPRENTICE

CHRIS RIDDELL

Drawing the Lie Tree for a Billboard Poster

...endless tendrils

← pastel Pencils

4th October — 2016 —

Remembering my younger self as I talk to students at my old Art school — UNIVERSITY BRIGHTON

5th October — 2016 —

Drawing while Poets read their work at the South Bank for NATIONAL POETRY DAY

one of my favourite things to do

6th October — 2016 —

THIS IS ONE OF MY FAVOURITE POEMS FROM ONE OF MY FAVOURITE POETS →

O ROSE THOU ART SICK.
THE INVISIBLE WORM,
THAT FLIES IN THE NIGHT
IN THE HOWLING STORM:

HAS FOUND OUT THY BED
OF CRIMSON JOY:

AND HIS DARK
SECRET
LOVE

DOES THY
LIFE
DESTROY.

William
Blake.

Showing off my medals
at the YLG conference
Dinner in
Cardiff...

shameless
basking

LIBRARIAN
LOVE

not
proud of
myself.

7th
October
-2016-

Taking the waters at
the Bath Festival of
Children's
Literature.

8th
October
-2016-

Wonderful
Children's
Book
authors and
Illustrators...

David
Roberts
Axel scheffler
Andy Stanton
Abie Longstaff
Katherine
Rundell

Frances
Hardinge

Ross
Collins

Maya
Leonard

9th
October
-2016-

at the
Cheltenham
Festival of
Literature

254

VISITING
THE
DREAMING
SPIRES
OF
OXFORD
WITH
Paul Stewart

10th
OCTOBER
— 2016 —

I GOT A DOUBLE FIRST IN DRAWING BIG NOSES...

Attempting to draw Jeremy Corbyn at an event at the House of Commons for All Party Parliamentary groups on Art, Design & Music.

Hosted by
The Big Draw
Campaign for drawing

11th
October
— 2016 —

Signing copies of 'The Lie Tree' with Frances Hardinge, drawing ~~Tony Robinson~~ Baldrick from 'Blackadder', having lunch with Phil Hogan of The Observer and writing thoughts on school library provision for Lord Bird, then—

Helping the Arts Council with their enquiries...

I MUST HAVE DONE IT - IT'S IN THE LAUREATE LOG...

Vol. V.

12TH October
— 2016 —

Vol. I   Vol. II   Vol. III   Vol. IV.

ENDING THE DAY ON A CROWDED TRAIN ILLUSTRATING A NEIL GAIMAN POEM.

Letter writing to very special people and making Laureate plans...

15TH October
— 2016 —

256

Drawing Jonathan Swift and his imaginary worlds

for the Literary Review

16th October
—2016—

LITERARY REVIEW

NOVEMBER 2016 Issue #48 £3.95

Jonathan Swift's Outrageous World
Freya Johnston

RASPUTIN'S REIGN
Donald Rayfield

CAPABILITY BROWN IN BLOOM
Tim Richardson

SCOOP OF THE CENTURY
Kate Adie

AGE OF ATTLEE
Paul Addison

TIME PIECES • NAZIS ON GUERNSEY • KNAUSGAARD UP FRONT
THE HORSE'S TALE • DRACULA DISSECTED • HAIRY BUSINESS

Nope...
I'LL DRAW INSTEAD

Attempting to write...
not quite managing to.

17th October
—2016—

18th October
—2016—

Stepping into the embrace of a new project

257

100 Hugs

Hoping the Donald has met his match...

drawing my cartoon for The Observer

21st October - 2016 -

NUANNAPOQ

NUANNAPOQ

Inuit -
the extravagant
pleasure of
being
Alive.

#Island
by
Nicky Singer

Sunday
Sketching

23rd
October
- 2016 -

AN ILLUSTRATION
FROM
'ISLAND'
BY
NICKY SINGER

Discussing Goth Girl
the Opera

with

Orlando
Gough the
composer
and
Stephen
Plaice
the
librettist

AND WE CAN
HAVE A CROCODILE
CHORUS...

MY
SITTING
ROOM
IN
BRIGHTON

24th October
- 2016 -

263

JACKIE KAY   EMILY BERRY   WILLIAM SIEGHART   DON PATERSON   SUSANNAH HERBERT

Let's throw this open to the audience...

Are modern poets obscure on purpose?

JACKIE KAY

DON PATERSON

Sketching poets at the Forward prizes for poetry event at the British Library 25th October -2016-

EMILY BERRY

SUSANNAH HERBERT

WILLIAM SIEGHART

All dressed up at Buckingham Palace for the Commonwealth Essay Competition Awards Ceremony

I'M BUSY FINDING OUT.

Gold Blue Peter Badge

Laureate Medal

Feathered Cap

Order of the Bathtime

Night of the Garter

Asked by the Dean of Westminster Abbey what a children's laureate is...

26TH October
-2016-

Listening to Radio Three as I draw in my Norfolk studio...

28th October
-2016-

In Norfolk

Writing and dreaming about what lies at the bottom of the Edge cliff...

27th October
-2016-

Showing off my very sharp pastel pencils at the Lavenham Children's Festival in beautiful Suffolk

29th October
-2016-

On a fantastical voyage into the depths...

#The Edge Chronicles

30th October
-2016-

Returning from Norfolk to Brighton on All Hallows eve

candle powered brain

Sharp as a witch's hat

← Zombie dance

31st October
-2016-

1st November

There'll be fireworks!

Discovering what lies at the very bottom of the Edge Cliff...

Who'd have thought...

2nd November
-2016-

Drawing
Embraces...

3rd
November
-2016-

IL PUCE

I'M GOING TO MAKE AMERICA WHITE AGAIN.

Having TRUMPMARES

Drawing my Observer Cartoon

4th November — 2016 —

Raising my voice at the Save Our Libraries demonstration at the British Library

HOW DO YOU STRENGTHEN LIBRARIES? YOU CELEBRATE THEM...

then talking books at #lovetoread event

5th November — 2016 —

268

Enjoying Pizza
in Swindon with
the two Steves...

Barlow

Skidmore

6th November
-2016-

Drawing
And
talking
At
the Swindon
Youth
Festival

*Brilliant
Week long
Book event
reaching
9,000
pupils
organised by
School
Librarians!

7th November -2016-

Having a Wonderful
time in Wales

At
Newport
Riverside
and

Cardiff
Waterstones
and
The Central
Library, Cardiff

8th
November
-2016-

Thankyou
Literature Wales!

...AND THEN
I GOT HOME
TO FIND OUT
THAT DONALD
TRUMP HAD
BEEN ELECTED
AS THE 45TH
PRESIDENT
OF THE UNITED
STATES

WHAT JUST HAPPENED ?

TRVMPMARE

9TH November
-2016-

Enjoying storytime with the great Michael Morpurgo at the J.M. Barrie lifetime achievement award

War Horse

10th November —2016—

Jacqueline Wilson   Me

Sketch book sharing with talented young graphic artists at the launch of 'BRIGHTON'S GRAPHIC WAR'

11th November —2016—

19TH NOVEMBER —2016—

MY BRAND NEW DOCUMENT CAMERA AND PROJECTOR

Having a lovely time at the Ascel conference talking to librarians and reading a Neil Gaiman poem I illustrated on the train.

Off to BBC Breakfast to kick off my School library Campaign

GIDDY UP!

HUBRIS

Reading for pleasure, Reading for life.

13TH November —2016—

Taking to the air waves -
B.B.C. BREAKFAST,
Radio Four - FRONT ROW, BBC Radio
OXFORD, CORNWALL, NEWCASTLE, GLOUCESTERSHIRE,
LANCASHIRE, MANCHESTER,
SHROPSHIRE, SUSSEX,
TEES, KENT,
YORK, JERSEY,

about my
open
letter
to
Justine
Greening

14th November
- 2016 -

DEAR JUSTINE GREENING,

I AM WRITING TO YOU AS THE UK CHILDREN'S LAUREATE AND PASSIONATE ADVOCATE OF THE ROLE THAT SCHOOL LIBRARIES AND SCHOOL LIBRARIANS PLAY IN THE LIVES OF OUR CHILDREN. I HAVE SEEN PERSONALLY, IN MY SCHOOL VISITS UP AND DOWN THE COUNTRY, HOW THEY PROMOTE READING FOR PLEASURE, AND IN DOING SO, TURN PUPILS INTO AVID READERS.

I AM DEEPLY CONCERNED THAT THIS ROLE IS NOT FULLY APPRECIATED AND, WORSE, IS BEING UNDERMINED THROUGH LACK OF ECONOMIC AND INTELLECTUAL INVESTMENT. IN RECENT MONTHS TWO MAJOR SCHOOL LIBRARY SERVICES CLOSED IN DORSET AND BERKSHIRE AND YEAR AFTER YEAR THE SCHOOL LIBRARY ASSOCIATION LOSES MEMBERS AS SCHOOL LIBRARY PROVISION SHRINKS THROUGH LACK OF FUNDING.

THE ALL-PARTY PARLIAMENTARY GROUP ON LIBRARIES HAS ASKED YOUR DEPARTMENT TO GATHER STATISTICS ON SCHOOL LIBRARY PROVISION SO THAT THE EXTENT OF THIS PROBLEM CAN BE UNDERSTOOD. SO FAR, WITHOUT SUCCESS.

I AM ASKING YOU TO ACT ON THEIR REQUEST AND THEN, WITH THE SUPPORT OF OFSTED, TO SET OUT CLEAR STANDARDS FOR LIBRARY PROVISION THAT WILL END THIS DISADVANTAGEOUS SCHOOL LIBRARY LOTTERY THAT LIMITS MANY CHILDREN'S LIFE CHANCES.
I AM ASKING YOU TO RING-FENCE FUNDS FOR THIS FROM THE EDUCATION BUDGET SO THAT EVERY SCHOOL HAS A LIBRARY SERVICE IT CAN BE PROUD OF: BOOKS TO BORROW AND WHEREVER POSSIBLE A SCHOOL LIBRARIAN TO HELP CHILDREN CHOOSE.
BY TAKING THE LEAD IN ENGLAND I HOPE THE DEVOLVED EDUCATION AUTHORITIES THROUGHOUT THE REST OF THE UK WILL FOLLOW SUIT.

BY PROMOTING READING FOR PLEASURE, INTRODUCING OUR CHILDREN TO LIFE-CHANGING BOOKS AND TURNING THEM INTO LIFE-LONG READERS, SCHOOL LIBRARIES ARE A VITAL RESOURCE THAT MUST BE NURTURED.

MY FELLOW LAUREATES HAVE CHAMPIONED LIBRARIES IN MANY DIFFERENT WAYS AND THEY HAVE GENEROUSLY LENT ME THEIR SUPPORT.

WHEN EVERY PARENT KNOWS THE NAME OF THEIR CHILD'S FAVOURITE BOOK, AUTHOR AND, YES, SCHOOL LIBRARIAN AND CAN SHARE AND READ TOGETHER WITH THEIR CHILD THE BOOKS THEY BRING HOME,

WE KNOW LITERACY STANDARDS WILL SOAR AND WE'LL ALL BE RICHER.

YOURS SINCERELY,
CHRIS RIDDELL
UK CHILDREN'S LAUREATE
WITH THE SUPPORT OF
SIR QUENTIN BLAKE CBE
ANNE FINE OBE
MICHAEL MORPURGO OBE
MICHAEL ROSEN
ANTHONY BROWNE
DAME JACQUELINE WILSON
JULIA DONALDSON MBE
MALORIE BLACKMAN OBE

THIS IS THE LETTER I WROTE TO JUSTINE GREENING... SHE REPLIED AND SAID EVERYTHING WAS FINE

15th November -2016-

Using my new toy -
a wonderful document
camera so I can
draw live at schools
on
my
Laureate
tour...

St. George's school
Blackpool,
Cedar Mount
Academy,
GORTON,
Manchester.

Getting into my stride
in Bolton -
canon slade school
and Ladybridge
Primary

then
the
beautiful
Broadhurst
Bookshop
in
Southport

16th November
-2016-

Visiting
the
Astonishingly
beautiful
Liverpool
Central
Library

on my
Book Trust
Laureate
Tour

17th
NOVEMBER
-2016-

BREXIT MEANS...
BORIS

THERESA'S CHINA SHOP

FREE MOVEMENT OF PEOPLE IS BOLLOCKS! STOP YOUR TRUMP WHINGE-O-RAMA OR I'LL KNEE YOU IN YOUR PROSECCO EXPORTS.

RIDDELL
20-11-16

Drawing Boris the buffoon

For The Observer

18th November
-2016-

Resting on my laurels

#saturday rest.

19th November
-2016-

Giving a Bafta to animator Peter Western at The Roundhouse, Camden

extremely heavy!

20th November
—2016—

Finishing touches to my latest book

21st November
—2016—

Going through my daughter Katy's portfolio as she pl... her caree...

22nd November
— 2016 —

Visiting Bexleyheath Academy and talking to Wonderful staff and pupils

BA

← DOCUMENT CAMERA

Joyful day

23rd November
—2016—

Catching up with Paperwork...

feeling Zen-like

24th November
—2016—

Drawing the elephant in the room for my Observer cartoon

25TH November —2016—

Drawing Hans Christian Andersen's 'The Fir Tree' in a little homemade film on YouTube

26th November —2016—

Journeying
to
the very
Centre
of
the
Edge
World

The
Descenders

27th November
—2016—

A LONG HAIR GOBLIN
ACADEMIC FROM THE
LOFTUS OBSERVATORY
IN THE BLUE GREY
ROBES OF THE
NEW
SANCTAPHRAX
ACADEMIES.

GRENT
ONETUSK

FENDA
FULE-FANE

A FETTLE LEGGER
BOTANIST FROM
THE ACADEMY OF
EARTH STUDIES
BASED IN
UNDERGARDEN.
SHE WEARS THE
BLUE GREY ROBES
WITH GREEN TRIM.

DENIZENS
KEEP

THE
GLISTER
FACE

THE SCREE
FIELDS

THE DEPTHS

AT THE VERY FARTHEST
REACHES OF THE DESCENDERS
RANGE, THIS IS THE MOST
DANGEROUS REGION OF THE
EDGE CLIFF. SHELTERING IN
THE LEE OF THE GREAT
OVERHANG, DENIZEN'S KEEP
PROVIDES AN ANCHORAGE FOR
THE NIGHT SHIPS. BELOW
IS THE GLISTER FACE, IMPOSSIBLE
TO DESCEND DUE TO THE
MIND ALTERING PROPERTIES OF
THE ROCK ITSELF. BELOW,
THE SCREE FIELDS DROP
AWAY INTO THE UNEXPLORED
BLACKNESS AND NIGHT SHIPS,
ON STRICTLY REGULATED
TETHERS, ARE THE ONLY
WAY THROUGH THEM.
INTREPID DENIZENS WORK
TIRELESSLY TO MAP AND
NAVIGATE ROUTES THROUGH
THE SCREE FIELDS AND
DOWN TOWARDS WHATEVER
LIES BELOW. A SNAPPED
TETHER CAN SPELL INSTANT
DEATH WHILST A GLISTER
STORM, A BEGUILING LIGHT
DISPLAY, CAN LEAD TO BLINDNESS
AND INSANITY.

A LEATHER BACKED
MUDCRAWLER FROM
THE NORTHERN REACHES

ALSO KNOWN AS
A SCUTTLEBRICK

ORIGINALLY DWELLING IN THE DEEP RAVINES BELOW
GORGETOWN IN THE NORTHERN REACHES, THESE
CREATURES HAVE BECOME DOMESTICATED AND ARE
USED BY THE QUARRY TROGS AS BEASTS OF BURDEN.
THEY ARE ALSO EXTREMELY ADEPT AT TRAVERSING
THE MUDDY AND TREACHEROUS TERRAIN OF THE AREA
NOW KNOWN AS THE GRASSLANDS OF THE MIRE.

A CLOUD CRUISER
from
The FOURTH AGE
of
FLIGHT

i. BEAKED PROW
ii. FLIGHT-PIT
iii. FORWARD PHRAX CANNON
iv. FLIGHT ROCK COILS
v. PHRAX ENGINE
vi. REAR PHRAX CANNON
vii. STEAM FUNNELS THRUST

A QUARRYTROG ACADEMIC FROM THE SCHOOL OF STONE STUDIES, THE ACADEMY OF EARTH STUDIES BASED IN THE STONE GARDENS AND HIGH CLIFF.

DEMORA DUSTE

A BLUE WAIF RAIN TASTER FROM THE ACADEMY OF CLOUD.

SENTAFRUICE

THESE ARE PAGES FROM THE BLACK SKETCHBOOK WHERE I MAKE ALL THE NOTES ON THE EDGE CHRONICLES — ONLY PAUL STEWART HAS EVER SEEN INSIDE BEFORE NOW

ACADEMICS OF NEW SANCTAPHRAX.

Visiting the wonderful Cartoon and Illustration Course at Wrexham Art School...

Extremely impressive work

lovely students

with Dan Berry, talented cartoonist and tutor

28th November
-2016-

Drawing and talking at Wrexham Library

Roby of BookTr

Zion, an enthusiastic member of my audience.

BookTrust Laureate Library Tour

29th November
-2016-

BookTrust Laureate Library Tour...

Bradford Library with Christinea then

Hebden Bridge 'The Book Case' Book shop with Kate

Emily of BookTrust

THIS IS A QUOTE I TOOK FROM THE GUARDIAN AND POSTED ON FACEBOOK WHERE FIVE MILLION PEOPLE READ IT

30th November
-2016-

A LIBRARY IS NOT JUST A REFERENCE SERVICE: IT IS A PLACE FOR THE VULNERABLE.

FROM THE ELDERLY GENTLEMAN WHOSE ONLY REMAINING HUMAN INTERACTION IS WITH LIBRARY STAFF, TO THE ISOLATED YOUNG MOTHER WHO RELISHES THE SUPPORT AND FRIENDSHIP THAT GROWS FROM A BABY RHYME TIME SESSION, TO A SLOW MOVING 30-SOMETHING WOMAN COLLECTING HER CDS,

LIBRARIES ARE A HAVEN

IN A WORLD WHERE COMMUNITY SERVICES ARE BEING GROUND DOWN TO NOTHING.

LIBRARIES ARE VITAL. THEIR WORTH CANNOT BE MEASURED IN BOOKS ALONE.

ANGELA CLARKE.

CHRIS RIDDELL

1ST
DECEMBER

RIVERSIDE
JUNIOR
SCHOOL
VISIT AND
FILMING
FOR
BBC BREAKFAST
FOR
BOXING
DAY.

– 2016 –

THE ELEPHANT
IN THE PARK

RIDDELL
4·12·16

Drawing a belligerent mouse
for The Observer...

2nd
December
—2016—

TORY MP
ZAC GOLDSMITH
LOST HIS SEAT
TO THE LIB
DEMS OVER
HIS SUPPORT
FOR BREXIT

SO, WHAT ARE THE CREATIVE ARTS FOR?
WHY MIGHT IT BE A GOOD IDEA TO SPEND
TIME ON THEM IN SCHOOLS?

THERE MIGHT NOT BE TIME FOR ARTS
UNLESS
YOU THINK THEY OFFER SOMETHING ELSE
SUCH AS
"A WAY OF INTERPRETING THE WORLD
THROUGH MAKING AND DOING."

IT FEELS FRESH, AND MAKES US SEE
OURSELVES IN NEW WAYS.

SO, WITH THE ARTS WE HAVE A METHOD
OF INTERPRETING THE WORLD THAT CAN
INCLUDE EVERYONE OF ALL AGES.
IF YOU THINK THIS IS IMPORTANT THEN YOU NEED
AN
"ALL ARTS FOR ALL" POLICY.

MICHAEL
ROSEN

CHRIS RIDDELL

My alter-ego
Sir Christopher
Riddle-of-the-Sphinx
expounding on

Fashion
at
the
V.&A.

with Rosie
Goldsmith
Fashion & Fiction
Talks

3rd
December
—2016—

I HEARTILY
AGREE WITH
MICHAEL
←

CHRIS PRIESTLEY IS
AN AUTHOR AND ARTIST
WHO I HAVE KNOWN
FOR OVER TWENTY-FIVE
YEARS. HERE HE IS,
APPEARING WITH ME
IN 'GOTH GIRL AND
THE WUTHERING FRIGHT'

SIR CHRISTOPHER
RIDDLE-OF-THE-SPHINX
R A

MR
CHRISTOPHER
PRIESTLEY

Off to
my
happy
place
at the
bottom
of
my
garden...

4th
December
—2016—

288

Drawing
Aliens for a
limited edition
Poster

5th December

— 2016 —

THE PRINT IS
CALLED 'THE
EXHIBIT' AND
YOU CAN SEE
IT OVER THE
PAGE

Colouring 'My Little Book of BIG FREEDOMS' for Amnesty
6th December -2016-

THIS IS THE COLOURFUL COVER

MY LITTLE BOOK OF BIG FREEDOMS

ILLUSTRATED BY CHRIS RIDDELL

Drawing a cycling Fish on the wall outside Downsbrook School's library during a visit to promote judging of The Blue Peter Book Awards.

- WORTHING -

8th December
- 2016 -

Drawing Boris as a muzzled sheep dog for The Observer this week

9th December

293

Turbulent times
in the
floating city

10th
December
- 2016 -

'THE DESCENDERS'
THE EDGE CHRONICLES

Reviewing the Sunday Papers
for 'Broadcasting House' on
Radio Four

...And in the Sunday
Sport, 'Killer spiders
in Xmas crackers -
millions could die
say Experts...'

11th December
- 2016 -

Being
photographed in
Narnia by the
Daily Telegraph
at

The
Story
Museum
OXFORD

12TH December
- 2016 -

Rehearsing
with
Martin ~~Oebelmann~~ Oelbermann
live drawing of

Under
Milk
Wood at

the
Jermyn St.
Theatre

13th December
- 2016 -

Talking to the Wise
Wizard Gaiman about

- * various
  things...

Very
exciting.

14th December
- 2016 -

I DREW THESE CHARACTER STUDIES
FOR THE BBC RADIO 4 ADAPTATION
OF 'STARDUST' BY NEIL GAIMAN

TRISTRAN
THORN
- STARDUST -

CHRIS
RIDDELL

THE
COPPER
BEECH
- STARDUST -

MORWANNEG
- STARDUST -

CHRIS
RIDDELL

VICTORIA
FORESTER
- STARDUST -

CHRIS
RIDDELL

CHRIS
RIDDELL

YVAINE

-STARDUST-

@HRIS RIDDELL

CAPTAIN ALBERIC

-STARDUST-

CHRIS RIDDELL

PRIMUS

-STARDUST-

SEPTIMUS

TERTIUS

CHRIS RIDDELL

-STARDUST-

QUINTUS

SEXTUS

SECUNDUS

QUARTUS

CHRIS RIDDELL

Entering the Fourth Age of Flight in The Edge Chronicles

'The Descenders'

15th December — 2016 —

A TALLOW HAT
STONE HARBOUR

A CLOUD CRUISER

THE TALLOWHATS USE ~~AND~~ FLIGHT ROCKS FROM ~~A~~ THE STONE GARDENS
TO CREATE STONE HARBOURS. TIMBER BUILT BUOYANT CABINS CALLED
LIGHT TOWERS ARE BUILT ON THE FLOATING ROCKS WHICH ARE CHAINED
IN CLUSTERS OF THREE, EACH WITH A BERTH FOR THE DISTINCTIVE
TALLOW HAT CLOUD CRUISERS. EACH CLUSTER IS CHAINED TO AN ANCHOR
POINT, USUALLY A PINNACLE IN THE ROCKY EDGE MARGINS. THE ~~ROCK~~
STONE HARBOURS CAN BE MOVED AND CLUSTERS ALTERED ACCORDING
TO SHIFTING TALLOW HAT ALLIANCES AND ~~BECAUSE~~ TO AVOID
DISCOVERY BY ENEMIES.

THE FASTEST PHRAX VESSELS EVER BUILT,
THE TALLOW HAT'S CLOUD CRUISERS HAVE
DISTINCTIVE 'BEAKED' PROWS AND PHRAX
GUNS MOUNTED IN THE ARMOURED BOW.
TWO TO FIVE PHRAX CHAMBERS DEPENDING
ON THE SIZE OF THE VESSEL ALL FEED THE
PROMINENT PROPULSION DUCT BELOW.
THE PRINCIPAL MODE OF ATTACK IS THE
CHARGING RAM, USUALLY TARGETING THE
WHEELHOUSE OF THE ENEMY VESSEL.

Wondering how Assad of Syria Sleeps at night for my Observer Cartoon 16TH December -2016-

Finished the last
chapter of the last of
the Edge Chronicles -
"The Descenders"

END OF
A
TWENTY
FIVE
YEAR
ERA

17TH
December
-2016-

Drawing
Polly Garter
and others from
Dylan Thomas'
"UNDER
MILK
WOOD"

18th
December
—2015—

Norfolk Christmas
Week begins...

#Big Sky Joy

19th
December
—2016—

AT THE OLD VIC THEATRE

Watching "ART" with Princess
Joanna of Norfolk

20TH December
—2016—

I HAD A MAD
WOODWORK
TEACHER WHO
TAUGHT US
COPPERPLATE
HANDWRITING BY
WHACKING US ON
THE KNUCKLES WITH
A CANE...

Drawing
with my
document
camera
and
projector
and

Talking to Home educators
at Catton Park, Norwich

21st December
—2016—

PRINCESS JOANNA of NORFOLK

I DREW THIS IN THE PAPERCHASE SKETCHBOOK
USING PASTEL PENCIL AND WHITE CHALK

Visiting Ada
at Ghastly-Gorm
Hall

Writing
"Goth Girl and
the Sinister
Symphony"

22nd
December
-2016-

Relaxing with
my Italian
sketchbook, drawing
in Pastel Pencil
and Blue pencil
crayon...

23rd
December
-2016-

PAPER PEOPLE PLACE
SETTINGS, CHRISTMAS
2016

Making
Paper people
place settings for
Christmas
Dinner.

Christmas
Eve
-2016-

ME

JACK

WILLIAM

PRINCESS JOANNA
of NORFOLK

KATY

OVER THE PAGE
ARE BLUE PENCIL-
CRAYON DRAWINGS
OF FEARSOME FAIRIES

CHRISTMAS DAY

ZZZZZZZ

Beautifully
Stuffed

CHRISTMAS
LICORICE

CHRISTMAS
SKETCHBOOK

CHRISTMAS
PENS

- 2016 -

BOXING
DAY

-2016-

Drawing my
New Year's Day
Cartoon for the
Observer...

Not a
great
6 year
politically

woolly
liberal
Leftie

30th December
— 2016 —

Macmillan would like to thank the following for permission to use copyright material:

pages 6, 8, 11, 25, 30–31, 33, 35, 38, 50–51, 55, 59, 74, 88–89, 93, 103, 120, 124, 126, 151, 156, 165, 168, 178, 185, 192–193, 208–209, 213, 220, 227, 235, 239, 241, 244, 256, 261, 268, 277, 279, 285, 293, 300, 312 © Chris Riddell, first published in the *Observer*

pages 9, 257 © Chris Riddell, first published in the *Literary Review*

pages 12–13, 232–233 © Chris Riddell, from *Odd and the Frost Giants* by Neil Gaiman, Bloomsbury Publishing plc 2016

page 15 from *Monster Slayer* by Brian Patten 2016, by permission of Barrington Stoke Ltd

page 17 © Chris Riddell, from *The Edge Chronicles: Doombringer* by Paul Stewart and Chris Riddell, Corgi Children's 2015

pages 18–19 © Chris Riddell, from *Dear Stranger*, Penguin 2015

page 21 © Chris Riddell, from *Island* by Nicky Singer, Caboodle Books 2015

pages 26, 128 'Face facts: we need fiction' © Neil Gaiman, first published in the *Guardian* 2013, by permission of Writers House Literary Agency on behalf of the author

pages 28–29 'The Way Things Are' © Roger McGough, from *Collected Poems*, Penguin 2003

pages 48–49 'Don't Squash' illustration © Chris Riddell 2015, from *A Great Big Cuddle* by Michael Rosen and illustrated by Chris Riddell. Reproduced by permission of Walker Books Ltd, London SE11 5HJ www.walker.co.uk

pages 63, 292 © Chris Riddell, from *My Little Book of Big Freedoms* classic edition, Buster Books 2017, in partnership with Amnesty International UK

pages 76–77 'Lesser Known But Not Less Important', from *Things You Find in a Poet's Beard*, Burning Eye Books 2015, © A. F. Harrold

pages 80–83 'Orphee' by Neil Gaiman, Headline 2015, by permission of Writers House Literary Agency on behalf of the author

page 96 © Chris Riddell, from *Something Else* by Kathryn Cave and Chris Riddell, Puffin 2011

pages 110–111 'Seven Dwarves' © Rachel Rooney

page 119 'Thirteen', from *Hold Your Own* by Kate Tempest, Picador 2014

pages 122–123 originally published in *Neverwhere* by Neil Gaiman with illustrations by Chris Riddell, text copyright © Neil Gaiman 1996, 1997, 2000, illustrations copyright © Chris Riddell 2016

pages 130–131 'The Scorpio Boys in the City of Lux Sing Their Strange Songs' by Neil Gaiman, from *Alan Moore: Portrait of an Extraordinary Gentleman*, ed. Smoky Man and Gary Spencer Millidge, Abiogenesis Press 2003, by permission of Writers House Literary Agency on behalf of the author

page 137 © Chris Riddell

pages 170–171 'The Minister for Exams', from *Armada*, HarperCollins 1996, © Brian Patten c/o Rogers, Coleridge & White, Literary Agents, 20 Powis Mews, London W11 1JN

pages 198–199 © Chris Riddell, from *The Sleeper and the Spindle* by Neil Gaiman, Bloomsbury Publishing plc 2014

page 273 © Chris Riddell, from *Brighton's Graphic War*, QueenSpark Books 2016

page 283 'A library is not just about books' © Angela Clarke, first published in the *Guardian* 2013

page 286 'Dear Justine Greening' © Michael Rosen, first published in the *Guardian* 2016

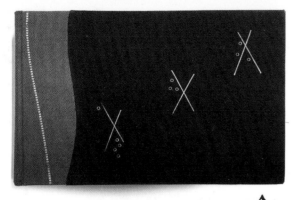

THE SKETCHBOOK ↗
MY MOTHER GAVE ME

MY

SKETCHBOOKS

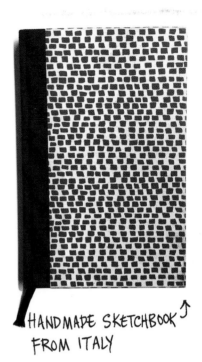

HANDMADE SKETCHBOOK ↗
FROM ITALY

THE BROWN PAPER SKETCHBOOK ↓

– CHRIS RIDDELL –

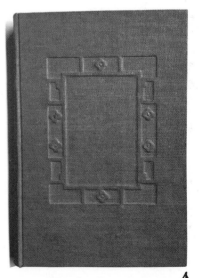

HANDMADE SKETCHBOOK ↗
FROM A LOCAL BOOKBINDER